CASE STUDIES IN ECONOMIC ANALYSIS

III

CASE STUDIES IN REGIONAL ECONOMICS

Kenneth J. Button
Lecturer in Economics
Loughborough University

and

David Gillingwater
Lecturer in Regional Planning
Loughborough University

Published by Heinemann Educational Books
on behalf of The Economics Association

Heinemann Educational Books Ltd
LONDON   EDINBURGH   MELBOURNE   AUCKLAND   TORONTO
HONG KONG   SINGAPORE   KUALA LUMPUR
IBADAN   NAIROBI   JOHANNESBURG
LUSAKA   NEW DELHI   KINGSTON

Students' edition ISBN 0 435 84090 8
Teacher's Guide ISBN 0 435 84091 6

© The Economics Association 1976

First published 1976

Published by Heinemann Educational Books Ltd
48 Charles Street, London W1X 8AH

Printed in Great Britain by
Cox & Wyman Ltd,
London, Fakenham and Reading

Case Studies in Economic Analysis

III

CASE STUDIES IN REGIONAL ECONOMICS

Economics Association Teaching Materials Project

CASE STUDIES IN ECONOMIC ANALYSIS

Series Editor : W. Peter J. Maunder

A series of detailed case studies designed to
enhance an understanding of real-world issues
for the student taking a degree course, professional
examination or Advanced level G.C.E. in Economics

1. *Case Studies in Competition Policy,* by Keith J. Blois, W. Stewart Howe and W. Peter J. Maunder
2. *Case Studies in Cost-Benefit Analysis,* by Kenneth J. Button and Peter J. Barker
3. *Case Studies in Regional Economics,* by Kenneth J. Button and David Gillingwater
4. *Case Studies in the Competitive Process,* by Peter J. Barker, Keith J. Blois, W. Stewart Howe, W. Peter J. Maunder and Michael J. Tighe

Contents

Introduction   1

1. The Regional Employment Premium   9
   A Particular Measure of Regional Policy

2. The Hunt Report on the Intermediate Areas   25
   Policy towards Grey Areas

3. The Strategic Plan for the North-West   40
   A Regional Plan for a Depressed Area

4. The Greater London Development Plan   59
   A Regional Plan for a Congested Area

5. The Regional Policy of the Common Market   73
   Regional Policy in Europe

In the *Teacher's Guide* only, Teachers' Notes begin on p. 93.

Introduction

The United Kingdom does not suffer from a regional problem; rather it suffers from a complex set of social, economic and political problems which are concentrated on a small number of administrative areas which over the years have come to be known as Standard Regions.

The primary object of this book is therefore to indicate just a few of these problems in the light of successive governments' attempts to relieve if not ultimately resolve them. The selection of case studies which follow is by no means exhaustive; the principal reason for their inclusion stems more from the nature of the policy rather than an assessment of the problems. Neither is the selection unbiased. The case studies were chosen as being broadly representative of the three principal strands of regional policy in this country: regional economic policy, regional strategic planning, and regional economic policy in the E.E.C.

Each case study – the Regional Employment Premium, the Report on the Intermediate Areas, the Strategic Plan for the North West, the Greater London Development Plan, and E.E.C. regional policy – attempts to spell out the policy problem in its context, to indicate its main features, to evaluate critically the usefulness of the proposals, and to outline contemporary comments on their general relevance.

THE CONTENTS OF THIS BOOK

The case studies contained in this volume cover a ten-year period from about 1965 to the present and try to capture the way regional policy has developed over this decade. The first two studies concern the principal strand of regional policy – regional economic policy – and they are, respectively, the Regional Employment Premium (R.E.P.) and the Report on the Intermediate Areas. R.E.P. represents perhaps the most significant development in regional policy since the famous Distribution of Industry Act of 1945. With its emphasis on subsidising labour rather than capital costs, and its across-the-board coverage, R.E.P. is also the most controversial contemporary policy in the promotion of regional development.

The second case study concerns the so-called Intermediate Areas, and in particular the deliberations by the Committee headed by Sir John Hunt. The Hunt Report is important because it represents an attempt to introduce a kind of sliding scale with respect to Assisted Area/rest of the country status.

The third and fourth case studies stress the other strand of regional policy – regional strategic planning. The first of these is the path-breaking *Strategic Plan for the North West* (S.P.N.W.). The S.P.N.W. is significant because it marks a substantial shift in emphasis and orientation away from its predecessors – the studies and strategies produced in the late sixties by the regional Economic Planning Councils. The emphasis in this case study is therefore on the logic underpinning the Joint Team's proposals.

The fourth case study concerns the now 'infamous' Greater London Development Plan. Of the strategic plans undertaken in the late sixties, the G.L.D.P. typifies the timeless and costless nature of strategic planning at that time. As a forerunner to the Development Plans currently being prepared by local planning authorities, the G.L.D.P. experience – in particular the inquiry in public which was largely responsible for its almost total dismantling and demolition – was salutary. If the G.L.D.P. débâcle finds its way into history, it will be as a turning point to mark the emergence of British strategic planning into the harsh world of politics.

The final case study is also the most contemporary: the development of regional policy in the European Economic Community. This study attempts to present the evolution of regional policy in the E.E.C. in the context of British thinking. Existing E.E.C. policy for the regions is outlined, together with the implications for the U.K. of the latest proposals.

The sources used are not new ones to exploit for case studies. What it is claimed is different about this selection is the rigour of each of the case studies in its selection of material, the questions set for discussion, and the preparation of Teacher's Notes. Not all case studies offer the 'answers' to qualitative questions or give notes bringing the reader up to date with events since the Report, Plan or Policy was published or judgement given. These studies offer both these aids in the Teacher's Guide published separately by Heinemann Educational Books.

REGIONAL PROBLEMS IN GREAT BRITAIN

It was stressed above that this book was concerned with social, economic and political problems viewed at a regional level, rather than with what has been called a regional problem. Since the case studies are more concerned with government policy in response to these problems, it makes sense to map out briefly what these problems might consist of.

Mr. Vivian Woodward, in an illuminating final chapter to the *Poverty Report 1974*, presents a particularly cogent picture of differences in what may be called levels of 'prosperity' between regions in this country.[1] He has selected three principal indicators: income, housing and health. The variations in income are given in rank order below (UK = 100):

Male unemployment rates – 127 per cent (i.e. South-East index 58; North index 185)

The proportion of workers in low-paid occupations – 75 per cent (i.e. South-East index 79; East Anglia 154)

Take-up of supplementary benefit – 56 per cent (i.e. South-East 81; North 137)

The number of households with less than half the average earnings for Great Britain as a whole – 36 per cent (i.e. South-East 82; Wales 118)

Proportion of females in employment – 31 per cent (i.e. Wales 77; South-East 108)

Proportion of the population over retirement age – 30 per cent (i.e. West Midlands 87; South-West 117)

Average household income *per capita* – 27 per cent (i.e. Wales 89; South-East 116)

Median earnings of adult males – 15 per cent (i.e. East Anglia 91; South-East 106)

Average earnings of male manual workers – 14 per cent (i.e. East Anglia 92; West Midlands 106)

Ratio of the lowest 10 per cent of male earnings to the median earnings for Great Britain as a whole – 12 per cent (i.e. East Anglia 94; West Midlands 106).

A crude analysis by the authors on these results indicates that it is possible to rank each region according to its performance with respect to these indicators. The ranking – from 'best' or 'worst' – is as follows: (1) South-East, (2) West Midlands, (3) East Midlands, (4) South-West, Yorkshire–Humberside, North-West, (7) East Anglia, (8) Scotland, (9) Wales, and (10) North. Which leads Woodward to conclude that, on the basis of these indicators: '. . . the proposition is that regional variations in male unemployment and employment rates and female employment rates are the most important facts of all from the policy point of view."

REGIONAL POLICY IN THE U.K. – CONTEMPORARY DEVELOPMENTS

Excluding regional policy in the E.E.C., British regional policy has developed along two distinct and, until very recently, very different paths. The first of these is the emphasis on regional economic policy – where the major interest focuses on economic and financial aspects associated with direct and indirect forms of assistance to individual firms and sectors. The second path is the emphasis on regional strategic planning – whose predominant interest focuses on the physical environment and its long-term management and development.

It is not the intention here to spell out either the historical development of regional policy in this country or the various measures in the armoury of regional policy. Both have been adequately outlined in Derek Lee's companion volume to this book, *Regional Planning and Location of Industry*.[2] Having briefly outlined the differences between the two strands of regional policy, it is proposed to outline the significant developments in regional policy since 1970. Nevertheless, it does seem necessary to emphasize two points: (a) the principal objectives of regional policy, and (b) the historical roots and contemporary basis of regional policy.

The four principal objectives of regional policy have been officially spelt out as follows:

(i) to avoid waste of manpower in the less prosperous areas;

(ii) to assist in obtaining a steady rate of economic growth;

(iii) to encourage a broader-based industrial structure in those areas too dependent on older and declining industries (so reducing excessive immigration), and

(iv) to provide part of a general planning strategy for each area in relation to population movements, industrial location and economic and social infrastructure.[3]

To these Derek Diamond has added two others: (a) the maintaining and strengthening of provincial cultures and identity, and (b) assisting in the achievement of a balance between population and environmental resources.[4]

It is also of relevance to note that the roots of regional policy extend back beyond the Special Areas Act of 1934 – the bench-mark identified by most writers as the beginnings of regional policy. In fact the roots of regional policy go back to at least 1910, with the setting-up of the Employment Exchanges and Employment Exchange Areas for the monitoring, assessment and channelling of labour supply and its matching to labour demand. However, the contemporary roots of regional policy must rest in the 1945 Distribution of Industry Act and latterly the 1966 Industrial Development Act. Up to 1970 it was the underpinnings of these two Acts which provided the basis of regional policy.

The situation post-1970 has been characterized by four significant developments, culminating in the Industry Act of 1972. The first development was rooted in the downfall of the Labour Government and the policy changes adopted by the incoming Conservative Government. In October 1970 the investment grant system under the 1966 Act was dismantled and replaced by tax allowances for manufacturing industry in the country as a whole. These were matched by five additional incentives to encourage development in the Assisted Areas:

(i) capital expenditure attracted free depreciation allowances, the range of which was also extended;

(ii) building grants were increased;

(iii) the financial limit on the amount of assistance payable to any one firm was raised, but related to the level of additional employment created;

(iv)   action under the Local Employment Act was made more flexible, e.g. increased grants and range of allowable infrastructure developments (transport, power, sewerage etc.);

(v)   grants for the clearance of derelict land were raised.

The second significant development came only four months later, in February 1971. On this occasion most of the incentives outlined above were extended and/or raised; Special Development Area status was broadened and extended to include the area around Glasgow and South Wales, and Tyneside was scheduled as an S.D.A. for the first time.

The third significant development was five months later in July 1971, when for the first time limited regional aid and financial inducements were offered to certain sectors of the service industry.

The fourth and most significant contemporary development occurred in March 1972 with the publication of the Conservative Government's White Paper entitled *Industrial and Regional Development*.[5] Later translated into the 1972 Industry Act, and incorporating provisions of the Local Employment Act, this White Paper was said to be the most wide-ranging and powerful Bill yet presented to Parliament concerning intervention by the State in industry and industrial affairs.

The provisions of this piece of legislation were three-fold: first, to set up a Minister for Industrial Development (under the Secretary of State for Trade and Industry), second, national provisions (primarily, improved tax allowances for capital expenditure irrespective of location) and third, regional provisions (the provision of regional development grants, i.e. cash payments for capital expenditure, for new plant, machinery, and buildings in S.D.As. and D.As. and buildings only in Intermediate Areas and Derelict Land Clearance Areas (see Map 1).

There are seven principal elements to these provisions:

  (i)   basic national incentives
 (ii)   basic regional incentives
(iii)   selective assistance
 (iv)   shipbuilding aid
  (v)   the setting up of an advisory Industrial Development Executive
 (vi)   re-employment and mobility of labour assistance
(vii)   policy for communications links with Europe.

Links between the two strands of regional policy – economic and strategic planning – were strengthened; co-ordination of action on the process of industrial regeneration in regions and the general planning of land use and physical resources were emphasized.

Having outlined the contemporary developments in regional policy, it is perhaps worthwhile commenting briefly on the situation pertaining

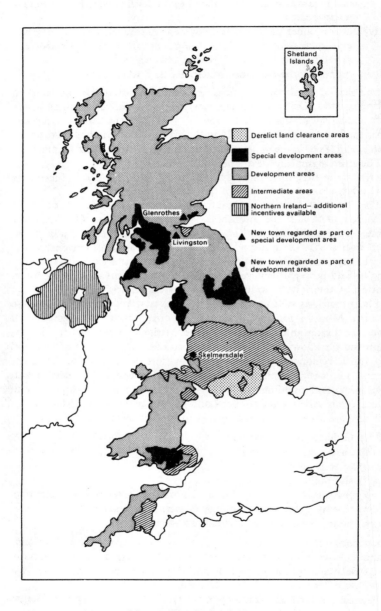

Map 1: The Assisted Areas.

to March 1976. With the Labour Government back in power, four developments of potential significance have been intimated. First, the Regional Employment Premium – which was under sentence of death by the Conservative Government – was reprieved and extended indefinitely in June 1974. Second, the 1972 Industry Act is still the basis of the Labour Government's regional policy. Third, and stemming from the latter point, the regional roles of the proposed State Holding Company along the lines of the Italian I.R.I. – the National Enterprise Board – and the autonomous Development Agencies proposed and established for Scotland and Wales. Finally, the uncertainty surrounding the nature and scope of regional devolution – ranging from limited administrative devolution to democratically elected regional Parliaments.

In conclusion, it would seem of relevance to outline some of the principal findings of a recent Parliamentary Trade and Industry Sub-Committee on regional development incentives.[6] These findings are basically:

(a) regional financial incentives have seldom instigated major new investment programmes and yet they would appear to have had a measurable impact in terms of the influencing of locational decisions;

(b) their main advantage seems to be in the offsetting of the higher operating costs associated with an Assisted Area location, or in improving profitability in these locations – 'a marginal bonus rather than a vital element';

(c) smaller firms seem to be influenced more by regional incentives than larger firms;

(d) few firms appear to evaluate systematically the magnitude or potential impact of the incentives on their operations, and consider them even less in making location decisions.

These conclusions led the Sub-Committee to make some of the most outspoken and critical comments ever levelled against contemporary regional policy. For example:

> Much has been spent and much may well have been wasted. Regional policy has been empiricism run mad, a game of hit-and-miss, played with more enthusiasm than success. We do not doubt the good intentions, the devotion even, of many of those who have struggled over the years to relieve the human consequences of regional disparities. We regret that their efforts have not been better sustained by the proper evaluation of the costs and benefits of policies pursued.[6]

CONCLUDING COMMENTS

This then sets the context for the five case studies which follow. In each there are four parts. Firstly, there is the material extracted from the principal source. Then follow about ten questions requiring the student to think around the facts and issues contained in the case study. In the Teacher's Guide further information on the background to the studies is provided. There then follow some suggested 'Answers' to the questions. These are not meant to be exhaustive, but simply to cover the major 'Points intended to be raised from the questions' – the title of the last section of each case study.

The diagnostic powers required for using these studies are those possessed by capable Advanced Level students. However, it is students reading Economics at degree level for whom these studies are essentially written. Students preparing for the finals of professional examinations may hopefully also find them of use.

The structure of these case studies for undergraduate use has been designed and edited by Peter Maunder.

NOTES AND REFERENCES

1. V. Woodward, 'The regional dimension', *Poverty Report 1974* (Temple Smith, 1974).
2. D. Lee, *Regional Planning and Location of Industry* (Heinemann Educational Books, 1970). See also G. McCrone, *Regional Policy in Britain* (Allen and Unwin, 1969).
3. C.O.I., *Regional Development in Britain* (H.M.S.O., 1974).
4. D. R. Diamond, 'The long-term view of regional policy', in M. Sant (ed.), *Regional Policy and Planning for Europe* (Saxon House, 1974).
5. D.T.I., *Industrial and Regional Development*, Cmnd. 4942. (H.M.S.O., 1972).
6. House of Commons, *Regional Development Incentives*, Second Report Expenditure Committee, Trade and Industry Sub-Committee, HC.85 (H.M.S.O., 1973).

The Regional Employment Premium
A particular measure of regional policy

The Regional Employment Premium (R.E.P.) – a subsidy to lower the cost of labour in the Development Areas – represents one of the most significant developments in regional policy since the 1945 Distribution of Industry Act. This case study attempts to explain and comment upon four aspects of its development. First, to explain why R.E.P. is important; second, to account for its development as a major strand of regional policy; third, to explain what R.E.P. attempts to achieve – its objectives and role; and finally, to assess its general utility and impact.

From the beginning the Government clearly intended R.E.P. to be a major plank of regional policy. As Michael Stewart, then Secretary of State for Economic Affairs, remarked in the House of Commons on 5 April 1967:

> I wish to make clear that the public presentation of this proposal is an initiative to which the Government attach great importance, because of the high priority which they give to a reduction of the disparity in unemployment levels between the development areas and the rest of Britain and to the achievement of the maximum rate of economic growth consistent with the maintenance of the stability and balance of the economy both internally and externally.[1]

The Regional Employment Premium is therefore important for four reasons. First, it marked an important political innovation. The proposal for R.E.P. was published, not as a Government White Paper, but as a Green Paper. *The Development Areas: A Proposal for a Regional Employment Premium*, published on 5 April 1967, was an advisory policy document for public discussion and consultation.[2] It represented an evolving view by government of policy for the regions rather than a concrete proposal. This form of presentation has since become a permanent feature of the presentation of many government proposals. Second, the publication of the Green Paper also marked a considerable administrative innovation. R.E.P. represented a substantial joint effort on the part of two separate and independent government departments, the now-defunct Department of Economic Affairs (D.E.A.), the ministry responsible for the long-term management of the economy (five to twenty years ahead), and the Treasury, responsible for short-term management (up to five years ahead) and the holder of the all-important purse strings of government. Given the conflict of interest which this split evoked, the joint proposal seems all the more impressive.

Third, it marked two significant changes in government attitudes to regional policy. For the first time in the history of regional policy one strand was to be directed solely at labour, and in particular a subsidy aimed at reducing the cost of labour in the Development Areas (D.As.). Up to this time the principal means of giving teeth to regional policy was in the provision of subsidies to capital – to reduce capital costs. The proposal for R.E.P. suggested that these capital subsidies should be supplemented by a parallel and independent scheme directed at reducing labour costs. Fourth, the second significant change was in the Government's attitude to firms already established in the Development Areas. It should be remembered that up to 1967 the principal means of effecting regional policy was designed to bring work to the workers: to tempt firms outside the D.As. to expand and/or relocate in them. But this policy excluded firms already located and established in the Development Areas from participating in and receiving the benefits of assistance.

THE CONTEXT OF R.E.P.

The Labour Government, elected in 1964 with a perilously small Parliamentary majority, was a government committed to the principal policy of raising the rate of national economic growth through a system of centralized economic planning (under the auspices of a new Department of Economic Affairs); and committed to a radical reassessment of the nature and role of regional policy, with a view to its potential strengthening.

The regional factor became an increasingly important aspect of government economic policy for the nation as a whole. It was already accepted in Whitehall that the promotion of discriminating regional policies could help in the bid for increased national economic growth, as the National Economic Development Council pointed out in 1963.[3] That the Government was committed to a strengthening of regional policy and a reduction in unemployment differentials between regions, simply reinforced and buttressed the quest for growth argument. The Regional Employment Premium was therefore but one part of this broader package, albeit a vital, additional and innovatory one. In many respects – and as a reading of the original Green Paper admirably illustrates – it was difficult to separate out precisely what the R.E.P. proposal would and would not achieve, it was so bound up with the broader export-led growth package.

R.E.P. IN OUTLINE

The problem which R.E.P. was designed to tackle was the matching of labour supply more satisfactorily to labour demand. The diagnosis was that an excess supply of labour existed in the Development Areas, a condition which was seen to be both persistent and recurrent.

Up to 1967 a partial solution to this mismatch was seen to lie in the implementing of regional policies to subsidize the capital costs of firms setting up production in manufacturing in the Development Areas. The assumption behind this indirect approach was that every additional firm would contribute to the creation of additional jobs in the D.As. This automatic gain, it was assumed, would be matched by a corresponding reduction in the demand for labour in the South and Midlands. Each job created in the D.As., whether as a result of an enforced move from a region experiencing excess demand or of new enterprise, was seen as tapping the source of the problem of excess labour – other things being equal. That this also happened to be to the benefit of reducing differentials in rates of unemployment between regions was a primary objective, but of secondary importance with respect to the actual implementation of regional policy.

By 1967 the problem of the relevance and matching of regional policy to national economic policies and their implementation was being critically examined. As the Green Paper puts it, the existing and expanded capital-oriented policies under the 1966 Industrial Development Act were deemed to be insufficient in resolving the problems of the Development Areas, particularly with respect to the more effective matching of the demand for and supply of labour. In assessing this gap between what was intended and what was resulting – or rather what was not resulting – the Government engineered the proposal for a Regional Employment Premium: a flat-rate cash payment to firms for every employee, male or female, full or part-time, trainees or trained, young or old. These flat-rate payments would be in addition to existing regional aid – the grants and other assistance for capital investment under the 1966 Act. Furthermore, they would apply exclusively to firms in the manufacturing industry. In short, the proposal was to be nothing more than an across-the-board wage subsidy to labour in those regions defined as experiencing conditions of excess supply.

As a subsidy to labour, the intention was that it would in effect reduce the direct costs of labour to industrialists. So long as the subsidy was recognized and deployed by industrialists in this way, each firm participating in the scheme could be capable of *either* employing the same size labour force, but passing on the subsidy element to consumers in the form of lower priced output (short-run, increasing competitiveness of product strategy) *or* maintaining price of output, but passing on the subsidy element to creating additional jobs (long-run, average cost reduction strategy) *or* attempt to do both – a mix of short- and long-run strategies.

What are the options open to the industrialist with respect to making use of this type of subsidy? Besides the three strategies outlined above there are clearly at least two others – *either* to employ the same size labour force at current wage rates, hold price of output constant, and pass on the subsidy element in the form of additional profit (short-run, profit maximizing strategy) *or* to pass on the subsidy element in the form of higher wages (short-run, labour holding strategy). However, if the industrialist considers the implications of this simple model it can be seen that by using the subsidy to create additional jobs, additional subsidy will be paid for them also. And in the creation of these additional jobs the excess supply of labour will be tapped, thereby reducing the level of unemployment in the Development Areas and the cost to the Government of unemployment benefit. Depending on the respective elasticities of demand for and supply of labour, so long as the total cost of the labour subsidy is less than or equal to the total cost of unemployment and other state benefits, then, other things being equal, the payment of a direct subsidy to labour is politically, if not economically, efficient.

Such was the thinking behind the Regional Employment Premium. The Green Paper pointed out that it would be directed at the realization of thirteen basic objectives:

1. To reduce disparities in unemployment levels between Development Areas and the rest of Britain.
2. To enable firms in Development Areas to increase their competitiveness by reducing costs *vis-à-vis* internal and external trade.
3. To create a more conducive atmosphere for firms already in Development Areas to increase both output and employment.
4. To create an additional inducement for firms contemplating a move to or setting up in the Development Areas.
5. To reduce pressures of excess demand for labour in the South and Midlands, reducing the well-known inflationary effects and damage to the balance of payments.
6. To reduce the condition of excess supply of labour in Development Areas.
7. To create an additional inducement for firms in Development Areas to increase investment programmes.
8. To create an additional inducement for firms in Development Areas to improve the quality of their products and/or sales promotion capacity.
9. To create an additional inducement for firms in Development

Areas to promote training programmes for new and existing employees.

10. To concentrate additional inducements in manufacturing industry, the sector with a predominantly export role and favourable multiplier effects.
11. To commit government to maintaining the subsidy for a minimum period, thus assuring industrialists the scheme would not be easily abandoned.
12. To minimize direct resource costs to the Exchequer.
13. To minimize costs of its administration.

From a consideration of the philosophy behind R.E.P., the objectives and role set for it, it would appear that it extends a significant way beyond being a simple labour subsidy. As the Green Paper pointed out, the proposal rested on three primarily economic propositions:

First, that the efficient management of the economy and the optimum use of manpower require major new measures to be taken to produce a more even distribution of industrial development as between the different regions, and as a result to secure a further substantial narrowing of the unemployment gap between the Development Areas and the rest of Britain;
Second, that the proposed regional employment premium would have this effect over a period of years, and that there are no practicable alternatives which by themselves could be expected to do so on the same scale;
Third, that provided these payments are confined to manufacturing industry in the Development Areas – their effects on the pressure of demand and the balance of payments will not be such as to require off-setting taxation to release resources for the subsidy.

In other words, it was assumed that (a) additional policy was required to supplement existing regional policy measures, moreover it should be of new and major proportions; (b) that a R.E.P. labour-based policy was the only permissible answer in response to the economic problems which the Government were experiencing and anticipating; and (c) that this type of major new policy would pay off only in the middle- to long-term, but would not contribute to exacerbating an already inflating economy running an imports surplus.

In the original Green Paper it was proposed that a premium should be paid to an employer in the manufacturing sector, already established in a Development Area, of between £1 and £2 per man per week for the duration of the scheme (three to five years) 'with appropriately smaller amounts for women, girls and boys'. The problem of part-time workers 'would have to be considered'.[2] On D.E.A./Treasury estimates this level of across-the-board subsidy would amount to a reduction of about 5–10 per cent of total labour costs in manufacturing industry in the Development Areas. Taking an average of £1.50p. (i.e. $7\frac{1}{2}$ per cent) this would, it was estimated, amount to total payments of about £100 million per year – at 1966–7 prices.[5]

The costs of the administrative machinery to organize and operate the scheme would be minimal, since machinery existed under previous legislation, the now repealed Selective Employment Payments Act of 1966. As a result of this Act all employers had to pay a flat-rate tax (S.E.T.) on each of their employees of 37½p. per full-time equivalent man per week. All employers in manufacturing industry, irrespective of where their plant was established, had to pay this tax, only to receive it back again with an additional payment – Selective Employment Premium (S.E.P.) – of 37½p. per man per week. The proposal for R.E.P. was therefore to supplement existing S.E.T. machinery. As the Green Paper commented: 'With a premium of the size indicated . . . the average disparity between unemployment in the Development Areas and the country as a whole might be reduced by something like one-half over a period of years, over and above the degree of success expected from existing programmes.'[2]

The proposal for a Regional Employment Premium then promised many things. The White Paper, entitled 'The Development Areas: Regional Employment Premium',[4] in many respects represented a more soberly, less emotive document than the original Green Paper. Presented again by a joint effort between the D.E.A. and the Treasury, it opened with a review of the argument of the Green Paper, a summary of the principal comments received, and the Government's conclusion. This was supplemented by an analysis and refutation of the main criticisms.

The Government's response was affirmative; the argument presented in the Green Paper was considered sound, the needs of the Development Areas being 'so pressing that they would be justified in introducing at an early date the Regional Employment Premium scheme for the Development Areas'.[4] This scheme would consist of seven main provisions:

1. The premium would be paid at £1.50p. per week per full-time male employee in manufacturing.
2. Corresponding rates for women and boys would be 75p. and girls 47½p.
3. Rates for part-time employees (between 8 and 21 hours per week) would attract half those for full-time employees.
4. To qualify the establishment would have to be wholly within a Development Area.
5. Payments would begin from 4th September 1967.
6. Payments at the proposed levels would continue either until 'their purpose has been achieved' or for not less than seven years in the existing Development Areas.
7. It would be implemented by means of an additional Clause in the 1967 Finance Bill.

CRITICISMS OF R.E.P.

The principal comments and criticisms levelled at the proposal and summarized in the White Paper were dealt with under eight general headings: the leak to higher wages; the leak to higher profits; the problem of branch firms; the need for additional taxation; alternatives to R.E.P.; the problem of labour shortage and training; R.E.P. as a blanket subsidy; and the exclusion of service industries.

Firstly, the probability that a significant proportion of the subsidy would filter its way through to higher wages was considered to be 'slight'.[4] Three reasons were given: (a) most changes in standard wage rates are negotiated nationally; (b) the existence of a pool of unemployed; and (c) both employers and trade unionists 'have a clear interest in co-operating'[4] to ensure that the scheme works.

Secondly, the White Paper conceded that some firms would – at least in the short-run – not reduce prices, but pass on the subsidy in the form of additional profit. The emphasis would be predominantly short-run because: 'There is considerable evidence that ultimately a cut in "prime" costs, which labour costs largely are, is passed on in manufacturers' prices, just as a rise in money wages is also likely to be passed on.'[4]

The third criticism concerned the problem of branches of national firms in the Development Areas. In particular that the subsidy would filter its way through to headquarters and not result in either cost or price reduction, price levels being determined nationally. The White Paper's counter-argument was that the subsidy could appreciably alter the relative profitability of those branches. The net result could lead to a re-allocation and expansion of production between factories in their favour, thus contributing to a reduction in the potentially inflationary excess demand situation in the rest of the country at the same time tapping the excess supply of labour problem in the D.As.

The fourth area of criticism concerned two aspects of taxation. The first was the response to the widely canvassed view that an R.E.P. type scheme would not be self-financing and would require the raising of additional public funds to pay for it. The reply was brief, pointed, and in the context of the times the orthodox Treasury view: '... in Britain today the objectives which determine how much taxation should be raised relate to the pressure of demand on domestic resources and the balance of external payments, not the crude relationship between the yield of taxation and Government outlay.'[4]

The second and more important argument on taxation was the criticism that if there was a substantial leakage into higher wages and profits, R.E.P. would not necessarily increase national output, but merely exacerbate the general pressure of national demand. This pressure would be most acute in the more prosperous non-Development Areas, i.e. the

South and Midlands, and the Government would need to take strong evasive action, primarily by increasing the level of taxation. The White Paper's counter-argument was (a) that any increase in national output would arise primarily in the Development Areas, with the result (b) that output in the rest of the country would most likely fall marginally, because (c) R.E.P., 'by lowering the costs of labour in the Development Areas relatively to the rest of the country, will shift some of the demand for manufactures from the present areas of high labour demand to the areas with a labour surplus'.[4] The crucially important factor was seen to be the inflationary danger of the pressure of demand in the more prosperous areas. Since this was likely to be reduced by R.E.P., 'it follows that no general increase in taxation is called for'.[4]

The fifth counter-argument in the White Paper concerned the criticism that R.E.P. was not as viable a scheme as competing alternatives. The White Paper disagreed, stating that the distinguishing feature of R.E.P. compared to others costing roughly the same amount was precisely that these alternatives were inflationary. A policy of increasing the level of public investment in infrastructure, e.g. by building more roads, would 'invariably mean a net increase in output in the areas where the pressure of demand is already high and, therefore, require a compensating increase in general taxation or a reduction in other forms of public expenditure'.[4] In other words, although the pool of local unemployment would be tapped, materials and services would more than likely have to be imported from the rest of the country. Moreover, this would contribute to inflationary tendencies because the damage in the short-run would have occurred before the long-run benefits of the policy had borne fruit, i.e. in attracting additional firms to establish themselves in the Development Areas as a result of this additional investment in infrastructure.

The sixth area of criticism to which the White Paper addressed itself was the view that R.E.P. would fail as a policy to increase the Development Areas' share of the national market because there was a lack of suitable labour, particularly in the skilled and semi-skilled trades.

The White Paper did concede that there could well be a problem in matching existing skills to the demands of an expanding manufacturing industry, but the White Paper put forward the view that these were problems where a labour subsidy like R.E.P. could be used to more than supplement existing government sponsored training programmes. It was precisely because of these potential bottlenecks, 'that have so often occurred in more prosperous regions',[4] that employers would be encouraged to promote their own training and retraining schemes.

The seventh counter-argument concerned the probable industrial effects of R.E.P. In particular, the criticisms that (a) it is wrong to subsidize all employees in all manufacturing firms in the Development Areas 'irrespective of their likely contribution to the areas' economic future'[4], and (b) subsidizing labour across the board simply props up firms which are inefficient users of labour and allows them to remain in business. In the former case it was argued that R.E.P. would favour labour-intensive rather than capital-intensive firms, the assumption being that in order to maximize a region's contribution to national economic growth it would be better to be selective, concentrating capital investment in high growth, capital-intensive firms. The Government's reply was that it would be 'misleading to equate capital-intensive industries with technologically advanced industry or to believe that the former are the only growth industries of the future'[4]. The electronics industry was cited as an example.

The view that an across-the-board subsidy would keep inefficient firms in business was countered by an argument which stressed that this would only arise if the firms in question did not make use of the subsidy to reduce their competitiveness.

The final counter-argument in the White Paper concerned the criticism that the Government was doing little to aid firms in the service industries in Development Areas. The reply was that the decision to concentrate on manufacturing was deliberate; most service industries are in local rather than national competition, and dependent to a large extent on servicing local manufacturing industry or their employees as consumers. An extension of the subsidy to include services would not result primarily in the capture of business from the rest of the country – a principal aim of the R.E.P. policy. Instead it would increase spending power in the Development Areas via the multiplier, and increase imports with inflationary results. The Government believed that the multiplier effects of R.E.P. itself would be of direct benefit to the service industry.

IMPACT OF R.E.P.

The White Paper was enacted by means of the promised new clause in the 1967 Finance Bill, and the scheme was launched with effect from 4 September 1967. The Conservative Party in Opposition opposed it through all of its Parliamentary stages, with the spectre of repeal if and when they were elected. A Conservative Government was elected in 1970, and the promise was repeated up to the presentation and passing of the 1972 Industry Act. The intention was that R.E.P. would die a natural death when the seven-year experimental period ended on 4 September 1974. But the General Election of March 1974 saw the return of a Labour Government and the almost immediate promise that R.E.P. would be reprieved and indeed strengthened. In June 1974 the Department of Industry issued the statement that R.E.P. would be doubled, from £1.50p. to £3 per full-time man per week (with similar increases for women, boys, girls, etc.), and would continue at least until a reassessment of policy for the regions was drafted and presented to Parliament.

It is necessary to consider the effect of the policy, and to assess whether its actual impact has measured up to what was originally intended for it.

The available evidence has emerged from four principal and published sources. Two are reports published as a result of academic research, the third consists of evidence presented by individual firms to a House of Commons Expenditure Sub-Committee on regional development incentives, and the fourth the pertinent findings of that Sub-Committee.

The research by Professor A. J. Brown[6] represents one of the earliest attempts to estimate the actual rather than the probable impact of the Regional Employment Premium. Writing in 1972, he attempted to assess the effect in three broad areas: (a) the impact on investment, (b) the impact on wage levels, and (c) the impact on employment levels.

The impact on investment in the Development Areas was, to use Professor Brown's words, in the event not conspicuous. The evidence of the diversion of firms and establishments to the Development Areas indicated: '. . . that it may have had a small and rapid effect, but this seems on the face of it to have faded out, or been countered by some unidentified influence tending to shift investment away from those Areas from mid-1968 onwards.'[6]

The impact on wages, and in particular the hypothesis that the subsidy would leak into higher wages, was considered by comparing the averages of hourly earnings in different regions, weighted to eliminate the effects of the different regional industrial structures. The conclusions which Brown reached were (a) that in recent years (1960–9) the Development Areas did improve their position with respect to the average for the United Kingdom, and (b) that this improvement, from October 1967 to the end of 1969, was of the order of about 1 per cent. The role of R.E.P. in this improvement is, however, not clear. As Brown remarked: 'relative improvement of earnings in the most heavily assisted regions seems to date mainly from a time well before the Regional Employment Premium . . . There is little sign of leakage here.'[6]

The attempt to assess the impact on employment was tackled in three stages. The first involved a simple inspection of the trends in mid-year estimates of employment in the regions from the late 1950s to 1969. This indicated that, as a proportion of the total employees in the U.K., the percentage of employees in the North, Scotland, Wales and Northern Ireland had fallen rapidly from 1958 until 1963, partly recovered and remained constant until 1965, but then declined again. From 1967–9 it held firm once more.

The second and third stages involved a statistical analysis of whether these changes, and in particular growth rates in employment in manufacturing industries between 1965–7 and 1967–9, varied in the Development Areas and in the rest of the country. The results of this analysis were far from conclusive, but they did show that the non-Development Areas achieved lower rates of growth than the South-East, which in turn achieved a lower rate of growth than the Development Areas. The exception was the North, which achieved the same performance as the South-East. As Professor Brown concluded: 'This is a broad indication that something, which may have been the Regional Employment Premium, improved the relative fortunes of the Development Areas.'[6]

The third stage involved the translation of the size of these differentials into actual numbers of employees. The results indicated that the Development Areas showed an improvement of about 31,000 and the non-Development Areas a deterioration of about 55,000 jobs. Professor Brown's conclusion was unequivocal:

> The literal, though naive, interpretation is that something (possibly the Regional Employment Premium) shifted the bias of growth in favour of the high-unemployment regions to the extent, over the period in question, of about 86,000 . . . With all allowance for the limitations of this test, it looks as if, from about the time of the introduction of the Regional Employment Premium, there was an improvement in the relative fortunes of the assisted regions . . .[6]

The analysis by Moore and Rhodes contrasts directly with that of Professor Brown. It is therefore not surprising that their results also differ. Their concern was likewise with the assessment of regional policy in general, and they too gave consideration to the likely cost and number of jobs created or preserved by R.E.P., but in the first three full years of its existence, 1968–70. The difference between the two approaches lies in Moore and Rhodes' attempt to separate out more systematically the impact of R.E.P. from the total impact of regional policy.

Firstly, they estimated what employment levels would have been in manufacturing in the Development Areas (basically Scotland, Wales, the North and Northern Ireland) had the regions' industries' growth in employment been at national rather than regional rates, over the period 1950–71. These 'expected' levels of employment could, therefore, be interpreted as likely employment levels had a regional policy not been implemented. Secondly, these 'expected' levels were then compared with what actually occurred over the period – the 'actual' levels. Thirdly, any differences between 'actual' and 'expected' levels could be interpreted as the impact of regional policy in the Development Areas. According to this analysis the differential between 'actual' and 'expected' levels of employment in manufacturing in the Development Areas was of the order of 12 per cent by 1971.

In their attempts to disentangle the impact of R.E.P. from these estimates, Moore and Rhodes argue that the gap between 'actual' and 'expected' employment levels widened after 1967 – the year R.E.P. was introduced. The problem is to assess how much of this gap R.E.P. was responsible for. They present three alternative interpretations to 'indicate strength of policy rather than obtain a precise measure'.[7]

First, if it is assumed that all non-R.E.P. policies failed – or rather were wholly ineffective – after 1967, the total impact of R.E.P. was probably of the order of 75,000 jobs in manufacturing in the Development Areas between 1968 to 1970.

Second, if it is assumed that these non-R.E.P. policies were as effective after 1967 as they were between the period 1963–7, then the R.E.P. impact is lower, probably of the order of 54,000 jobs over the three years to 1970, of which the impact of R.E.P. was probably as low as 20,000 jobs.

The third interpretation is a more refined version of the second. It concerns the problem of lead- and lag-time, i.e. the time period between the implementation of a policy and when it begins to have a measurable effect.

Moore and Rhodes considered a lag-time of about eighteen months as a reasonable average estimate for all industry. On this assumption the impact of R.E.P. would probably be of the order of 27,000 additional jobs in the Development Areas. However, to this figure must be added:

(a) The effect of R.E.P. in shipbuilding and metal manufacture (which were excluded from the original calculations because of the bias they would have introduced into the estimates) – about 5,000 jobs.

(b) The effect of R.E.P. in the two Development Areas of Merseyside and the South-West (which were also excluded from the original calculations) – about 7,000 jobs.

(c) The multiplier effects in the service industries in the Development Areas which could have been expected as a result of the increase in jobs in the manufacturing sector – about 5,000 jobs.

This increases the original estimate from about 27,000 jobs to a combined total estimate of 45,000 jobs in the years 1968–70.

For the corresponding period the total R.E.P. payments were £53 million for 1968, £122 million for 1969 and £129 million for 1970, at current prices and gross of tax clawback (excluding Merseyside and the South-West D.As.). Moore and Rhodes estimated that as a percentage of average earnings (a measure of the size of the subsidy) this represented 6·5 per cent in 1968, 7·6 per cent in 1969 and 6·7 per cent in 1970. (For 1971 their estimate places the size of subsidy at less than 5 per cent.) Nonetheless their concluding remarks, like Professor Brown's, were unequivocal. Writing at the time when the policy was under sentence of death, they argued:

Although our measure of the effects of R.E.P. as indicated by the available evidence is perhaps below what the Labour Government expected of it, the total abolition of R.E.P., which has provided or preserved a large number of jobs in areas of high unemployment which would not otherwise have been there, could have quite serious adverse consequences for the Development Areas.[7]

THE VIEWS OF R.E.P. RECIPIENTS

The views of manufacturing firms in receipt of the subsidy are equally unequivocal, but split between those who considered R.E.P. a valuable form of assistance, and those who considered it to be largely irrelevant.[8]

In evidence to the Trade and Industry Sub-Committee, Chrysler considered R.E.P. to be an important feature of government policy, going some way to compensate for 'the adverse economic factors affecting employment in assisted areas'. G.K.N. were of a similar opinion – a labour subsidy was one of the easiest ways 'to compensate for annual running cost disabilities'. Unilever, whilst unable to quantify the impact of R.E.P. on their operations, considered that a labour subsidy of limited duration was important but could be tied more specifically to the creation of 'new' jobs. Wilkinson Sword suggested that 'assistance in the form of a payment related to employment' was of considerable importance. Vauxhall and Plessey were of a similar opinion, but suggested it should be 'geared to operating costs' for the former and 'linked to levels of employment' for the latter. Dunlop considered R.E.P. was important because it was a direct form of assistance, unlike most incentives (e.g. interest-free loans, depreciation allowances, etc.), 'of great value as an offset to the higher cost of inexperienced labour'. Philips were of the opinion that R.E.P. had been a useful form of direct assistance, if not the best from their operating point of view; alternative policies of direct assistance were possible, and 'not necessarily related to employment levels'. Honeywell suggested that any proposal to remove or lower the subsidy without compensation would probably affect their profits more than prices, and in any case would need to 'be offset by its value being made available in some other form'.

Ford and Reliant were the only two companies to give explicit mention of the relationship between R.E.P. and its impact on setting up new plant in the Development Areas. Ford considered the subsidy to be a particularly useful form of aid 'which went some way to offset the financial penalties of location dispersal, and which should be continued in some form or another'. Reliant were of a similar opinion, R.E.P. being 'one of the constructive ways of offsetting the additional costs of relocation'.

In the words of the Sub-Committee's Report, three other firms thought a little differently. For Burroughs, R.E.P. was relatively insignificant as a financial incentive – 'a bonus rather than a critical part of the equation'. For their labour-intensive production they operated in low wage-earning countries like Taiwan and Hong Kong. The problem of R.E.P. for I.B.M. was its uncertain future. While it clearly figured in their operations, they included it only on a heavily discounted (i.e. short-run) basis. Courtaulds were of the opinion that R.E.P. would never be a significant form of assistance in their operations. Their estimate was that the subsidy contributed to 1 per cent or less on their returns 'compared with 7 per cent on grants, as between assisted and non-assisted areas'.

The C.B.I. took a middle course, claiming that R.E.P. was both a good and a bad thing. On the one hand, for large firms they considered the subsidy was treated as more of a windfall than a significant factor in decision-making. On the other hand it was an integral feature of the financial structure of many firms. In principle, the C.B.I. were not in favour of R.E.P. As an across-the-board subsidy it assisted inefficient as well as efficient operations. Nevertheless, it should be maintained and extended to include the service sector at least until the end of 1978 to give short-term continuity and reduce uncertainty about its future.

The evidence submitted on behalf of the T.U.C. was admitted as being impressionistic. In their estimation R.E.P. was a necessary operational subsidy, a third to a half of which was used to reduce prices, a third to increase profits, and a sixth to a third to increase earnings[9]. Moreover, it was also a policy which appeared to achieve direct and beneficial results in both the maintenance and creation of jobs in the Development Areas. Like the C.B.I. they agreed that the subsidy should be extended to include the service industries.

The fourth and final area of critical comment on the impact of R.E.P. concerns the findings and conclusions of the Trade and Industry Sub-Committee. The pertinent paragraph on R.E.P., which also concluded in unequivocal terms, ran as follows:

Our evidence suggested that many firms locating in development areas had come to rely on R.E.P. as an important factor in their profitability, offsetting not so much the initial extra costs of labour in a new location as what they considered to be the continuing financial disadvantages of operating in a remote area. R.E.P. is a stronger incentive to employment than to investment, but in the absence of a thorough quantitative evaluation of its effects it is difficult to judge whether or not there could be more effective ways of spending £100 million in a year ... The middle estimate of 45,000 jobs in three years implies a cost-per-job figure of between £6,000 and £7,000, which is about the same as (the) overall cost-per-job figure for all regional incentive expenditure over the period 1963–70 ... Our evidence however left us in little doubt that the withdrawal of R.E.P. without any comparable replacement could create operating difficulties for many firms.[8]

NOTES AND REFERENCES

1. *Hansard*, House of Commons Debates, Vol. 5 April 1967, Col. 245.
2. D.E.A./H.M. Treasury, *The Development Areas – A Proposal for a Regional Employment Premium*, H.M.S.O., 1967.
3. N.E.D.C., *Conditions Favourable to Faster Growth*, H.M.S.O., 1963.
4. D.E.A./H.M. Treasury, *The Development Areas – Regional Employment Premium*, Cmnd. 3310, H.M.S.O., 1967.
5. In November 1967 an estimate was presented to Parliament that in a full year receipts would amount to £40 million for Scotland, £28 million for the Northern D.A., £18 million for the North-West D.A., £12 million for Wales and £1·6 million for the South-West D.A., *Hansard*, 9 November.
6. A. J. Brown, *The Framework of Regional Economics in the United Kingdom*, N.I.E.S.R.-C.U.P., 1972.
7. B. Moore and J. Rhodes, 'Evaluating the Effects of British Regional Economic Policy, *Economic Journal*, Vol. 83, March 1973, pp. 87–110.
8. House of Commons, *Regional Development Incentives*, Second Report Expenditure Committee, Trade and Industry Sub-Committee, HC. 85, H.M.S.O., 1973.
9. Compare with (a) Moore and Rhodes' estimates of 50 per cent to price reductions, 40 per cent to increased profits, and 10 per cent to higher wages (quoted in [7]); (b) Treasury estimates of 20 per cent to higher wages and 80 per cent to price reductions (quoted by Brown [6]).

QUESTIONS FOR DISCUSSION

1. How does R.E.P. differ from traditional types of regional policy?
2. Summarize the principal criticisms levelled against R.E.P.
3. What were the provisions of R.E.P. as outlined in the White Paper? How do they differ from (a) the original proposal and (b) current provisions?
4. Draw diagrams to show how a subsidy to the cost of labour tackles the problem of reducing the excess supply of labour in the Development Areas? (This is an application of supply and demand analysis.)
5. Discuss some of the reasons why evidence as to the impact of R.E.P. is patchy and inconclusive.
6. Outline and compare the actual uses of R.E.P. made by firms. How do these compare with the uses suggested by theory?
7. What are the alternatives to R.E.P.? Discuss their advantages and disadvantages.

8. What are the likely effects of a high rate of inflation on the value and importance of R.E.P.?
9. With respect to R.E.P., what do you understand by:
   (i) 'excess supply'; (ii) 'filtering'; (iii) 'lag-time'?
10. To what extent did R.E.P. depend on the Selective Employment Tax?

The Hunt Report on the Intermediate Areas
Policy towards grey areas

The Labour Government elected in 1964 was committed to achieving economic growth by means of national economic planning. Almost immediately upon election it established the Department of Economic Affairs and set about fulfilling its manifesto aim of 'Planning the New Britain' by drawing up a National Plan. As part of this policy they intended to improve the economic performance of the depressed areas of the country. Prior to 1964 economic assistance was available to specific Development Districts where unemployment exceeded 4–4½ per cent and incentives were offered to industry willing to establish or expand in such areas. This regional policy was subject to a number of criticisms (for an overview see [1]). Foremost amongst these was the feeling that the assisted areas were too limited in geographical area and that both the objectives of faster economic growth and the alleviation of regional pockets of unemployment could be more successfully pursued by extending the areas receiving assistance. It was claimed that the potential for growth was limited in many of the Development Districts but that the un-employed labour could be fruitfully employed by encouraging industry to locate at 'growth centres' near the pockets of unemployment where prospects were much better. There were also criticisms of the actual types of incentives in use which some people felt were inappropriate or inadequate for dealing with the regional problem.

Against this background the Labour Government's regional policy was formulated. As part of this policy new larger Development Areas were defined to replace the districts under the Industrial Development Act of 1966, and in the following year Special Development Areas were designated as in need of particular attention (specifically mentioned were areas where a decline in coalmining was creating high unemploy-ment). The policy itself can be divided into three broad strands. First, attempts were made to improve and strengthen infrastructure in the areas. Second, the Board of Trade tightened up its criteria for issuing Industrial Development Certificates (I.D.Cs.) (required for factory construction or major extensions of existing buildings) which discouraged firms settling in the already congested South-East and Midlands. Finally, various forms of inducements (carrots) were offered to entice industry to the assisted areas. These included the provision of investment grants of 40 per cent in the Development Areas (compared with 25 per cent elsewhere) to cover the cost of new plant and the introduction of direct employment subsidies (the Regional Employment Premium) after 1967. By 1967 the Development Areas and the Special Development Areas were benefiting to the tune of some £260 million per annum as a result of these policies.

The difficulty was that despite these measures there were still quite large areas of the country which, although difficult to define strictly as depressed, were nevertheless not prospering – the so-called 'grey areas'. It was these areas that a Royal Commission headed by Sir Joseph Hunt was commanded to consider. The Committee was appointed on 21 September 1967 and was charged:

> . . . to examine in relation to the economic welfare of the country as a whole and the needs of the development areas, the situation in other areas where the rate of economic growth gives cause (or may give cause) for concern, and to suggest whether revised policies to influence economic growth in such areas are desirable and, if so, what measures should be adopted.[2] (para. 1).

One of the earliest tasks was to define exactly where these 'grey areas' were; in all ten criteria were decided upon as significant. These were in order of importance:

(a) Sluggish or falling employment.   } Major indicators of
(b) A slow growth in personal incomes.   } slow growth
(c) A slow rate of addition to industry and commercial premises.
(d) Significant unemployment.
(e) Low or declining proportions of women at work.
(f) Low earnings.
(g) Heavy reliance on industries whose demand for labour was growing slowly or falling and was likely to continue to do so.
(h) Poor communications.
(i) Decaying or inadequate environment including dereliction.
(j) Serious net outward migration.

The problems of these regions were subsequently summarized by Professor A. J. Brown (who served on the Committee) as follows:

> At the second level of urgency come the grey areas dealt with by the Hunt Report, where employment growth is slow or in some cases negative, but net outward migration, usually assisted by a low rate of natural increase, is sufficient to prevent heavy overt unemployment – though in some cases there has been a fall or an abnormally low increase in activity rates.[3] (page 339).

Although not as obviously in need of assistance as the Development Areas these 'grey areas' represented a drain on the nation and did not contribute their full potential towards national economic growth. In addition, the pattern of labour migration meant that expansion in these areas could contribute to the reduction of congestion and overcrowding in London and the South-East region. Perhaps more importantly, it was felt that if no action was taken to alleviate the immediate problems of the grey areas there could well be a cumulative decline in their economies resulting in further outward migrations of labour and a continuing slowing down in growth rates – skilled workers would migrate leaving the less dynamic behind, while capital would not be replaced as it became obsolete or worn out.

The regional policy being pursued in 1967 did not help these grey areas and in many ways contributed to their difficulties. They did not possess the natural economic advantages of the South-East or Midlands, yet were expected to compete on the same terms as these regions for the investment which was not being attracted by regional incentives to the Development and Special Development Areas. Regional policy at the time may have been effective in diverting capital from the congested to depressed regions, but it was also diverting it from the grey areas. Specifically, the Economic Planning Councils for the North-West, Yorkshire and Humberside and the South-West complained in 1966 that the regional measures introduced in that year would have adverse effects on their local economies. There were also general fears that the introduction of the Regional Employment Premium (R.E.P.) then under discussion, would compound the problem.

The Committee which was finally formed comprised nine men, including one economist (Professor A. J. Brown), the remainder included planners, trade unionists and businessmen. The overall approach it adopted was to address itself to the identification of what it took 'to be causes of concern as measured by a wide range of economic and social criteria' in the grey areas or, as they were subsequently named, Intermediate Areas. The Committee presented a Report of some 250 pages in April 1969, nineteen months after being appointed. Although all members signed the final report, included in their findings were several 'Notes of Dissent' which showed individuals' reservations about some of the recommendations. Some of these notes attracted as much attention as the Report itself.

THE REGIONAL PROBLEMS

Before considering the particular problems of the Intermediate Areas the Committee felt it expedient to learn as much about the effectiveness of the different types of regional policy tools then in use as possible. This task they took upon themselves despite its omission from their terms of reference. Their interest was practical; in order to recommend policies for the Intermediate Areas they had first to assess the effectiveness and power of the alternative policy instruments available. In one sense the timing of the inquiry was unfortunate because the Regional Employment Premium (combined with Selective Employment Tax (S.E.T.)) was introduced in September 1967, only some two weeks before they set to work. This meant that they could neither appraise its usefulness as a policy tool in the Intermediate Areas nor assess the impact on these regions of its introduction in the Development Areas.

The Committee expressed particular concern about the deep-rooted nature of the regional problem and seemed rather unimpressed about the success of past policies in finding a long-term solution. In 1968 the unemployment in the Development Areas was still 4·1 per cent of the male working force, compared with an average of 1·9 per cent over the remainder of the country. Although recognizing that much of the problem was due to declining demand for the products of several basic industries, the Committee also noted the inadequate communications into many of the depressed areas.

An examination in detail of the effectiveness of alternative regional policies was made extremely difficult because of the lack of adequate regional accounts and statistics, although there was some indication that it was better to encourage 'growth points' within a region and to direct attention towards making these more attractive to investors, rather than to spread assistance thinly over the whole area. Encouraging industry to a particular area within a region generates so-called agglomeration economies (e.g. of large-scale production, marketing, transport etc.) and attracts further industry stimulating more rapid economic growth.

The Committee examined some rather suspect and incomplete information which the Board of Trade had collected from some 116 firms concerning their motives for selecting new locations in the period 1964–7. About half of the firms questioned selected sites within the Development Regions and some 86 per cent of these gave labour availability as one of the reasons for moving there. In terms of assessing government policy some 70 per cent said this had been a major influence on their decision and a further 15 per cent said it had been of minor importance. The grants for plant and machinery appeared as the most important single influence, although 20 per cent of firms also stated that the availability of government loans had played a part in the decision to move to a Development Area.

On the negative side, the Board of Trade's own Industrial Development Certificate policy had been only of minor significance, mainly because many of the sample had decided their location on the basis of the availability of existing buildings which did not come within the I.D.C. controls. On the other hand, the attitude of the local authority and the general quality of environment were of quite a high magnitude of importance in the location choice. Interestingly, access to supplies of materials or components or to existing branches of the firm were comparatively unimportant.

In summary, a large number of factors seemed to influence a firm's choice of region and its selection of a Development – as opposed to unassisted – Area, but the intra-regional choice was dominated by environmental considerations and the attitude of the local authorities and other promotional bodies.

The evidence, therefore, suggests that the depressed areas were benefiting to some extent from the regional policies of the time. The effect of these same policies on the grey areas was less clear, although as one later commentator has said:

> But the evidence certainly does not disprove the case made by the intermediate areas. That case must indeed be valid in the long run; if one asks the question, 'Under what theory about industrial location will a subsidy given to Liverpool be neutral in its effect as between Wigan and Croydon?' the answer is that there can be no such theory, except under the empty assumption that industrial location is totally random.[4] (page 250).

In other words any subsidy or assistance given to the Development Areas will attract industry from other regions. The areas most likely to be net losers are the relatively less attractive ones, such as Wigan (in a grey area) rather than ones which are reasonably attractive, such as Croydon (in the prosperous South-East). Consequently, it was argued, development assistance must take a hierarchical form, directly related to the unattractiveness of an area, if it is not going to operate to the detriment of the intermediate regions.

The Committee considered a number of different types of area which could require some form of economic assistance but were not within the boundaries of either Development or Special Development Areas. In all, four separate categories of such regions were defined. First, there were the traditional grey areas of the North-West and Yorkshire and Humberside where the existing regional policies were having adverse economic and social effects. Second, there were a number of older industrial areas which had not been given development status, e.g. Stoke-on-Trent, North Warwickshire, etc. Third, there were a number of areas directly bordering the assisted regions, e.g. parts of Wales, Edinburgh/Leith and the South-West. Finally, there were coastal and rural regions which were suffering from local unemployment problems.

The Committee took considerable trouble to assess the particular problems encountered in these areas and to look at policy alternatives. A large amount of evidence was put before them, some of it in private to enable detailed discussions to take place, but the lack of adequate statistics meant that much of it was of a qualitative rather than quantitative nature. The Committee also reviewed the situation in the South-

East and West Midlands in some detail – the economic vigour of these regions was thought 'vital to the economic welfare of the country as a whole' particularly because of their exporting potential. Any recommendations concerning the intermediate areas would have adverse effects on the growth in the South-East and West Midlands as it would mean diverting investment and jobs to the less dynamic grey areas. A delicate balance was thus clearly required.

HUNT'S RECOMMENDATIONS

Two important constraints were considered in the development of a set of principles upon which realistic recommendations might be based. First, the fastest growing sector in the U.K. economy was the service sector but this seemed to offer little assistance for the grey areas. Service sector industries were attracted to areas where there was already evidence of a firm economic foundation of manufacturing industry – the lack of this base was the very problem to be solved in the grey areas. This meant that policy recommendations were effectively limited to attracting manufacturing and processing industry, and this in turn offered no quick solution to the inadequate growth problem. It takes time for such industry to establish, due to high capital costs, and growth is slow. Second, the macro-economic situation prevailing in the country at the time of the inquiry was such that there was little prospect of substantial financial assistance being made available. The late 1960s was a period when the national balance of payments situation demanded a restraint on public expenditure. Financial stringency, therefore, both limited the range of policy tools available to the Committee and the number and size of regions they could realistically suggest assistance for. A compromise had to be reached between helping those areas in greatest need – which would be expensive for the probable improvements obtained – and assisting those with the greatest potential for economic growth. It was assumed by the Committee that assistance for the Development Areas would continue at the same level as before.

Of the areas with a claim to assistance, the Committee found that some had considerable scope for future development and growth (a 'geography of opportunity'), while others were run-down and unlikely to be attractive to investors (a 'geography of need'). Taking the constraints and the needs of the nation into consideration, the Committee decided that after the Development Areas, those regions where assistance could most profitably be given were Lancashire and Yorkshire. They showed 'many of the characteristics of slow growth on a substantial scale – a high proportion of industries with declining manpower, slow growth of employment, persistent net migration, below-average earnings and a poor environment'. As a consequence, they recommended that the North-West and Yorkshire and Humberside Economic Planning Regions be designated as Intermediate Areas.

The Report recognized the problem of certain other areas but decided that they were either less serious or less amenable to assistance than Lancashire and Yorkshire, although they would require watching in the future. As we see later, some limited assistance was recommended for these areas but resource limitations prevented substantial financial aid being made available. It was felt that to drain the West Midlands and the South-East of further investment would be 'costly to the national economy and in the long run even self defeating'. To this end the Committee considered that I.D.C. policy could be usefully modified.

The regions selected to become the official Intermediate Areas were large, embracing about 20 per cent of the population of Great Britain, and consequently there were considerable variations in the economic conditions within their boundaries, especially in the North-West Economic Planning Region. It was argued, however, that it would be wrong simply to concentrate aid solely on small areas where economic growth was slowest, and that a comprehensive policy of assistance applied to the regions in their entirety was desirable. (This recommendation was at least partly determined by the Committee's knowledge of the poor record of the earlier Development Districts.) The fact that this approach meant assisting already relatively prosperous regions was considered of secondary importance to attracting industry to the general area, leaving businessmen freedom to select the site offering the best prospect of long-term viability. It was hoped, however, that the additional creation of growth points within the various Intermediate Areas would eventually lead to spread effects and ultimately to economic growth in the whole region. A secondary, but not unimportant, motive was that administrative economies are possible if a small number of large areas are adopted for assistance rather than a multiplicity of smaller ones.

Assistance itself was to be through a number of different channels. These were summarized in a statement by Mr. Peter Shore, Secretary of State for Economic Affairs, in the House of Commons on 24 April 1969 (see also [5]):

1. The whole of the Yorkshire and Humberside and North West regions should qualify for an entirely new 25 per cent building grant not linked to the creation of new jobs. They should also qualify for training grants and direct training assistance on the same basis as in the Development Areas.
2. In selected growth zones within these regions there should also be Government estates and factory building with supporting investment including link roads.
3. For these two regions and in the Notts/Derby and North Staffordshire planning sub-divisions there should be an 85 per cent grant for derelict

land clearance as in the Development Areas. The clearance programme should be speeded up in all these areas and in the Development Areas.
4. The I.D.C. control should be relaxed throughout the country by raising the exemption to 10,000 square feet [from 3,000 sq. ft.].
5. The Merseyside Development Area should be de-scheduled and treated on the same basis as the rest of the North-West region.

These measures were seen as a package which, taken together, would have cumulative effects. The emphasis was not on attracting industry from other regions, although this was not entirely absent, but rather to regenerate and modernize that already in the Intermediate Areas. To this end the proposals were designed to improve the 'total environment', including not just that infrastructure immediately connected with industrial activity – roads, docks, railways, etc. – but also the whole network of urban, technical, educational and cultural facilities which have an important, but less direct, bearing on the long-term potential of a region. This emphasis on infrastructure, both industrial and social, was something of a departure from the regional policy pursued up until this time.

The underlying philosophy of modernization is reflected in the recommendation that the proposed building grant be paid to all industrial manufacturers in the Intermediate Areas and not exclusively to those creating immediate employment. (Two of the Committee expressed reservations on this particular aspect of the package, Sir Sadler Forster and Mr. M. J. C. Hutton Wilson. They felt that, 'inevitably there would be a waste of limited resources as a result of the payment of the building grant to some manufacturers whose production was not in line with current national needs. There would be no guarantee that the higher productivity which the Committee very properly wants to encourage would be achieved'.) The proposed land clearance grants also reinforced the basic emphasis on environmental improvement as an attraction to industry. The Committee found that some 93,000 acres of land in England were derelict, 20,000 acres in Wales and 17,000 acres in Scotland and this, it was argued, was depressing economic opportunity. The problem was particularly acute around the older coal-fields and it was felt that with the limited funds available effort should initially be concentrated there. In the long-term all such land should be cleared within fifteen years.

The proposal to reschedule Merseyside within the North-West Economic Planning Region rather than leave it as a Development Area was for another reason. It was felt that the Merseyside/Manchester belt was becoming congested and the need for overspill towns was becoming pressing. To continue with financial aid for firms settling in this area on the same scale as other Development Areas would only add to the congestion problem, especialy as many of the sites for overspill towns were outside Development Areas and consequently would find it difficult

to attract industry. As a consequence, the Committee felt that the distinction between Merseyside and the remainder of the region was no longer justified or desirable and that declassification would help alleviate the problems of congestion and overcrowding. (There may have been another reason for the proposed rescheduling of Merseyside, as A. J. Brown has pointed out, 'the descheduling of Merseyside . . . although it was never put that way, did just happen to pay for pretty well all the others'.[6])

I.D.C. reforms were thought extremely important. Evidence of their restricting growth in the South-East and West Midlands was presented by several bodies (e.g. the Confederation of British Industry and Birmingham Chamber of Commerce) but it was by no means conclusive. Official sources showed that some 17 per cent of firms applying for I.D.Cs. in the South-East and West Midlands had their applications refused between 1964 and 1967 but four-fifths of these firms found acceptable sites elsewhere. The difficulty with this type of analysis is that it does not reveal how many firms were deterred from applying for a certificate because they felt they had no chance of being awarded one. As one commentator has put it, how many firms were 'frightened away from non-development areas by informal Civil Service pressure, by way of hints that "*if* you are so foolish as to apply for an industrial development certificate there, of course you won't get it."'?[4] (page 249). The Hunt Committee did not feel that I.D.C. policy was undesirable in itself, but rather that some modification to the existing system would be beneficial – specifically in relation to the size of building involved and the availability of certificates in overspill and new towns regardless of their parent region. By raising the limit before I.D.Cs. became necessary, it was hoped to encourage the expansion of small firms which were frequently unfamiliar with official procedures. In the Intermediate Areas it was also suggested that I.D.Cs. be given unreservedly to new firms provided there was no acute labour shortage in the area.

PROFESSOR BROWN'S 'NOTES OF DISSENT'

Professor Brown felt that the specific recommendations of the Committee were 'generally helpful' but in a fairly substantial 'Note of Dissent' questioned some of the assumptions of the general approach and expressed reservations relating to certain particular recommendations. His main areas of concern were:

(a) The stress laid on improvement on 'infrastructure', as against use of fiscal and financial inducements, as a means of stimulating growth.

(b) The specific application of this to the intermediate areas.

(c) Doubts as to the readiness of Merseyside for so drastic a change as loss of development area status, and the effect of such a change on the North-West as a whole.

(d) The possible adverse effects of certain proposed measures on the development areas, and of some of them on the intermediate areas also.

(e) What seem to be the conclusions that should be drawn from the evidence presented concerning policy in the longer term.

Professor Brown opposed the use of the infrastructure strategy on two grounds. Firstly, it was too costly, 'committing some hundreds of millions to uses where their degree of utilisation is lower than it would be in other places'. Secondly, he felt the policy had doubtful drawing power for industry. The first point reflects Professor Brown's argument that infrastructure investment should take place where it is most beneficial, which is not necessarily in the Intermediate Areas. (This is a cost-effectiveness approach to social investment designed to maximize the return from a limited supply of investment funds.) If, as the Report seemed to suggest, the intention was to provide infrastructure in the Intermediate Areas superior to that in the rest of the country specifically to attract industry, then, Professor Brown argued, this would produce a lower direct contribution to real national income than if the funds were used somewhere else.

The argument put in favour of more direct assistance to industry via larger investment grants, is that their real cost to the country is minimal – grants representing transfer payments from taxpayer to industry. The only objection to this is that the taxpayer may be opposed to subsidizing industry but, in terms of efficiency, grants are a far more effective tool for encouraging mobile industry to settle in depressed areas than infrastructure improvements. This was reflected in the evidence of the Board of Trade mentioned earlier.

Professor Brown specifically felt that the need for financial incentives was even stronger in Lancashire and Yorkshire than elsewhere, the decline of coalmining and other industries being difficult to compensate for. The policy of infrastructure improvement and assistance to selected growth points was seen as inappropriate in areas which were not characterized by a scattered population seeking centres to concentrate, but rather by existing centres with adequate communications and infrastructure. Professor Brown argued that encouragement was needed for new firms to take over what already existed. Where problems were acute, such as at the Yorkshire coalfields, greater and more direct assistance was needed than the Report envisaged.

In addition to this, A. J. Brown did not feel the Merseyside area was ripe for descheduling, especially in view of the rapid population increase being experienced and the possibility of unemployment re-emerging. The inflow of industry into the area had not been at the expense of the rest of the North-West and descheduling was unlikely to mean that more industry would go to the rest of the Yorkshire–Lancashire area; it was more likely to go to some other Development Area.

Of the other measures, Professor Brown argued that the relaxation of I.D.C. policy and the recommendation that industry should be permitted to locate in overspill areas in preference to assisted areas would have considerable adverse effects on both the Development and Intermediate Areas. This was purely a matter of judgement, given the inadequacy of reliable data, but Professor Brown felt that if Merseyside was not descheduled (as he suggested) then the remaining Development Areas would not have an increased inflow of investment diverted from that source and consequently relaxation of I.D.C. controls in the South-East and West Midlands would not be adequately compensated for.

Professor Brown also felt that regional policy as a whole required some rethinking. In particular he had reservations about the imbalance between capital and labour employment incentives – policy being very much biased in favour of the former (this point is also emphasized by Hardie in his review of regional policy in the 1960s[1]). Additionally he seemed to advocate the creation of French-style regions with a spectrum of different categories of regions accompanied by a flexible set of policies. (Richardson[7] has subsequently suggested this could be improved upon by also limiting the range of policy tools applied but differentiating the rate at which the regions are assisted.) Professor Brown defined policies for four types of areas which would be appropriate in the U.K. context:

(a) For the Development Areas, a better balanced version of the existing incentives.
(b) For the Intermediate Areas, corresponding benefits at half these rates.
(c) For the rest of the country apart from congested areas, no benefits.
(d) For areas in more prosperous parts of the country where there is serious physical congestion as well as pressure on the labour market, a 'congestion tax' on all employment.

THE GOVERNMENT'S REACTION TO HUNT

The Government received the Hunt Report and then almost immediately introduced measures which ran directly counter to its recommendations. (This was done in Mr Peter Shore's speech cited earlier.) The Government's decision was partly political in nature, although it did suggest different economic priorities from those followed by Hunt. The Government's single criteria for assisting the Intermediate Areas was a rapid reduction in unemployment; the wider aims of Hunt were ignored or at least deemed inappropriate for the time. To this end the idea of building grants was rejected since modernization of existing industry did not necessarily guarantee more jobs immediately. Similarly, the proposal to assist the large Yorkshire and Humber side and North-West regions was rejected in favour of concentrated 'assistance to industry with an employment link on a strictly limited number of smaller areas ... the selection of areas to be given assistance to industry must be governed strictly by criteria of need, especially the level and character of unemployment and numbers of unemployed.' To this end the following broadly defined geographical areas were selected for assistance:

The Yorkshire coalfield area.
The Erewash Valley area of Derbyshire.
Parts of Humberside.
The main industrial areas of North-East Lancashire, east of the proposed New Town.
A substantial part of South-East Wales.
Leith.
Plymouth.

These areas were to be given three explicit types of assistance, namely:

(a) Grants at 25 per cent of factory building costs.
(b) Government-built factories (both custom-built and advance factories) on the same basis as in the Development Areas.
(c) The full range of Development Area training grants and other training assistance, together with assistance for the transfer of key workers.

In addition to these measures it was intended that there would be some extra expenditure on roads and encouragement with the provision of new housing in selected areas. Also grants to assist with derelict land clearance were proposed in the areas recommended by the Hunt Committee, although they were only to cover 75 per cent of the capital cost of clearance, compared with 85 per cent already being given in the Development and Special Development Areas.

Merseyside was not to be descheduled because of the serious 'structural problems' which persisted there. Nor did the Government accept the need to relax I.D.C. policy, although it did recognize a need to adopt a more flexible attitude in the case of industry wishing to locate in overspill and new towns where refusal to grant a certificate would slow the inflow of people from the exporting region or city.

SOME REVIEWS OF THE HUNT REPORT

The Hunt Report aroused considerable interest amongst both economists and regional planners and the Report was reviewed extensively in the learned journals.

Several reviewers were not simply concerned with the actual findings and recommendations of the Committee but questioned the usefulness of the inquiry itself. Charles Carter[4], for example, saw it as a method of enabling the Government 'to delay making up its mind' about the grey areas. This view was to some extent shared by Harry Richardson[7] who pointed out that by the time the Report was finally completed 'the steam had gone out of public pressure for more regional development measures'. The political motives underlying the setting up of the Committee are therefore in doubt.

The Hunt Committee was also handicapped in its work by the terms of reference within which it had to operate and by the total inadequacy of the regional statistics upon it was supposed to base its conclusions. The reviewers differed in their exact attitude to these problems. One view was that the terms of reference were far too wide and that it was rather optimistic to expect the Committee to 'view their prospects *in the widest possible* context, even if . . . this means taking in all the major economic and social issues of the day.'[9] It was simply impossible to look at everything as the terms seemed to imply. Another opinion, that of Richardson, was that the terms of reference were too restrictive and did not allow a full assessment of the effectiveness of past regional policies. A rather more balanced view is that of A. J. Odber[10] who, although recognizing the restrictiveness of the terms of reference, did not feel that they inhibited the inquiry to any great extent. Odber felt that the inadequacy of regional statistics was a far more stringent constraint on the activities of the Committee and that this led both to the opposed recommendations of the Report and Professor Brown's 'Note of Dissent' and to the rather preconceived ideas of the Government dominating the final legislation.

The timing of the inquiry was also unfortunate. The R.E.P. had just been introduced, which meant there was no time to appraise its effect on the regional situation, and in addition the Department of Economic Affairs, which had initiated the inquiry, was disbanded midway through the study and its responsibilities spread over several other government departments. In addition the task of the Committee was not made any easier by businessmen delaying their investment decisions whilst 'waiting for Hunt'. This meant that the actual existence of the Committee distorted the very problems it was attempting to investigate.

Despite the several difficulties besetting the Committee and the ultimate rejection of its recommendations by the Government, the Hunt

Report still served several useful purposes. The study discussed in detail the various policy instruments available to tackle the regional problem and set out their respective pros and cons, although a full review was beyond its terms of reference. It also shed valuable light on the particular problems of the Intermediate Areas. Finally, we might also point to a rather negative assessment of the contribution of the Hunt Report presented by Peter Self who concluded his review with the following rather cynical remark, 'Hunt is a disappointing document. Much can be learned from its mistakes however.'[11]

REFERENCES

1. J. Hardie, 'Regional Policy', in W. Beckerman (ed.), *The Labour Government's Economic Record 1964–1970*, Duckworth, 1972.
2. Department of Economic Affairs, *The Intermediate Areas*, H.M.S.O. Cmnd. 3998, 1969.
3. A. J. Brown, *The Framework of Regional Economics in the United Kingdom*, Cambridge University Press, 1972.
4. C. F. Carter, 'The Hunt Report', *Scottish Journal of Political Economy*, Vol. 16, November 1969, pp. 248–255.
5. 'The Intermediate Areas', Department of Economic Affairs, *Progress Report No. 52*, May 1969.
6. A. J. Brown, 'Thoughts on the Hunt Report', *Regional Studies Association, Conference Paper Manchester*, May 1969.
7. H. W. Richardson, 'The Hunt Report', *Yorkshire Bulletin of Economic and Social Research*, Vol. 22 November 1970, pp. 54–64.
8. 'Government proposals for intermediate areas', Department of Economic Affairs, *Progress Report No. 55*, August 1969.
9. G. M. Lomas, 'The Hunt Report: A Geographer/Planner's View', *Area*, No. 3, 1969.
10. A. J. Odber, 'Policy After Hunt', *Urban Studies*, Vol. 7, June 1970, pp. 205–8.
11. P. Self, 'Intermediate Areas', *Town and Country Planning*, Vol. 37, June 1969, pp. 242–6.

QUESTIONS FOR DISCUSSION

1. Why was it thought necessary to set up a Commission to look into the problems of the so-called grey areas? What were the main characteristics of these areas?
2. 'Official policy had placed too much emphasis on regions where unemployment was highest and this was creating long-term problems for the Intermediate Areas'. Explain.

3. What were the main attributes of the alternative instruments of regional policy at the time of the Hunt study? How successful were the various types of industrial incentives?

4. What were Professor Brown's main objections to the recommendations in the Report?

5. Give reasons why infrastructure improvements are often thought inferior to investment grants as a means of attracting industry to an area. Explain why you either accept or reject these reasons.

6. What were the main differences between the Report's recommendations and the measures introduced by the Government with respect to the Intermediate Areas?

7. In what ways was the Hunt Report a success? In what ways was it a failure?

8. Briefly explain why the Report made the following recommendations:
   (a) The de-scheduling of Merseyside.
   (b) The introduction of a new system of building grants.
   (c) Wider policies of derelict land clearance.

9. A. J. Odber has said: 'the Hunt Committee did an excellent job but was handicapped from the start.' Explain what he meant by this.

10. What modifications to I.D.C. policy did Hunt recommend? Why did Professor Brown object to these proposals and the Government finally reject them?

11. 'Regional assistance should be based upon a hierarchy of different categories of region each receiving the appropriate degree of help.' Why is this an oft-heard argument? What sort of hierarchy would you recommend?

The Strategic Plan for the North-West
A regional plan for a depressed area

As a case study the S.P.N.W. is important for at least four reasons.

First, it represents a good example of current best practice with respect to strategic planning at the regional level. It is therefore an example of another strand of government policy for regional development, with different administrative arrangements and objectives.

Second, the S.P.N.W. marks a significant move away from previously published strategic plans. Indeed it has paved the way for a radical rethink of the very role of regional strategic planning in government – on whose behalf such plans are prepared.

Third, it illustrates the basic conflicts between central and local government which characterize – and sometimes determine the fate of – such plans.

Finally, the North-West, as part Development Area (Merseyside) and part Intermediate Area, is an important region politically and economically, being the largest metropolitan region in the country outside London.

This case study is therefore concerned with illustrating each of these aspects, but within the framework of the S.P.N.W. itself. Two broad topics will be outlined and examined:

(a) The administrative context of the S.P.N.W. – the objectives of strategic planning, its organization and responsibilities, and terms of reference. In other words, what a strategic plan consists of.

(b) The S.P.N.W. itself – the problems which were identified, the objectives which were set for the region's development, together with recommendations and the preferred strategy.

BACKGROUND AND ADMINISTRATIVE CONTEXT

The *Strategic Plan for the North-West*, published in May 1974, represents the cumulative effort of about two years' work on the part of a Joint Planning Team.[1] Originally commissioned on 11 March 1971, the Report – of around 300 pages – was completed in July 1973. The ten-month delay led *The Guardian* to suggest that its publication was being held up for political reasons, pointing out a link between the imminent prospect of a General Election and the 'powerful ammunition' which the Report allegedly contained.[2]

The S.P.N.W. was commissioned jointly by the Government, the local planning authorities in the North-West, and the North-West Economic Planning Council, on what has come to be known as the tripartite principle. The strategy was prepared by a Joint Team staffed by officials seconded from the Department of the Environment (as the representative of central government and the department responsible for the strategic planning side of regional development policy), from Lancashire and Cheshire County Councils, and individuals recruited directly for the Team. A Consultative Committee was appointed to direct the work, and consisted of senior officials from central and local government. The Joint Team was directed by A. G. Powell, who until 1971 had been Deputy Director of the South-East Joint Planning Team.

The principal reason for this administrative arrangement was to insulate the Team from any specific vested interest, pressure or allegiance to any one organization. The time-consuming and public débâcle which led to the setting-up of the South-East team in 1969 set this particular precedent. The problem arose as a result of the attempt by the South-East Economic Planning Council to prepare and submit to government a strategy for the long-term future development of the South-East. As A. G. Powell has noted:

> The E.P.C. strategies were basically physical and aroused the immediate animosity of the statutory local planning authorities. This was notably the case in the South-East, where the planning authorities had associated themselves into a relatively powerful standing Conference ... In 1967 the South-East Economic Planning Council produced its *Strategy for the South-East* ... at a time when the Standing Conference was working towards a parallel, but possibly conflicting document.[3]

The main objectives of strategic planning at the regional level, as spelt out in the S.P.N.W., were two:

1. To guide decisions by central and local government on public expenditure and economic and social policies affecting the region.
2. To provide a context for the development plans of local planning authorities.

These objectives were reinforced by the four terms of reference under which the Joint Team had to operate:

(i) To consider and report with recommendations on patterns of development for the region, taking into account existing planning proposals with the aim of providing a strategic framework for the North-West.

(ii) To indicate a desired future pattern of social, environmental and economic development for the region, and to suggest policies for the solution of major, long-standing, physical planning issues of regional significance.

(iii) To submit to the Consultative Committee an issues report indicating (a) the main problems facing the region; (b) the proposed method of dealing with these problems – discussion of objectives, suggestions as to alternative strategies and proposals for their evaluation; and (c) recommendations about the form of a monitoring unit to take over after completion of the strategy.

(iv) the issues report to be submitted within six months, and the study as a whole to be completed in not more than eighteen months following the views of the Consultative Committee.

The principal objective of the strategy was, therefore, to build a platform and forge links between central government and local government and *vice versa*, in respect of what the Joint Team called matters of national concern (the creation and distribution of wealth and maintenance of national standards) and local concern (dealing with people and their needs, promoting and controlling development).

In attempting to build this platform the Joint Team had to contend with three basic constraints besides those of time and the Consultative Committee. They were required (a) to make the fullest use of existing studies of the region, (b) not to delay the Development Plan's work of the local planning authorities, and (c) not to impede major decisions already taken.

The substance of the *Strategic Plan* itself broadly follows and matches these demands. Divided into twelve chapters, the Report first of all outlines its basic approach, methodology, scope and assumptions. Attention is then paid to the problems of 'how much growth?', 'opportunities and needs', 'resources' and 'public expenditure priorities'. The emphasis then changes to specific functional aspects: 'the urban environment', 'employment policy', 'the regional transport policy', 'the regional open land policy', and 'the physical pattern of development'. The final part is given over to 'the meaning of the strategy' and to the problems of 'implementation and continuous planning'.

Approximately two years and four months after the Joint Team had been set up they were able to write: 'We consider that these requirements have been met; and, in general, we have been conscious of the need to temper idealism with realism.'[1]

THE STRATEGIC PLAN IN OUTLINE

The North-West region, illustrated in Figure 3.1, was first subjected to scrutiny by the regional Economic Planning Council in 1965. The *North-*

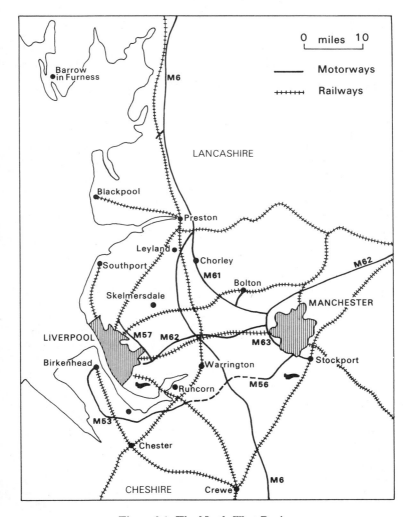

Figure 3.1. The North-West Region.

West: A Regional Study was one of the pioneers of regional strategic planning (Mark I) published under the auspices of the now defunct Department of Economic Affairs. This study was promptly followed up by a strategic plan (Mark II), entitled *North-West of the 1970s*, and published in 1968. The Government's response to this particular plan, in the light of the débâcle surrounding strategic planning in the South-East at that time, was predictable: the proposals were noted, and action would follow Government public spending plans. In practice the strategy was quietly shelved.

The reasons for the Government's selection and approval of the North-West for a Mark III strategic plan are unclear. Explanations have ranged from the intensive political lobbying on the part of the North-West Industrial Development Association, to the high proportion of members of the Cabinet and Members of Parliament in the North-West with 'an ear in the Cabinet'. But both are more akin to grand conspiracy theories than rational explanations.

One factor which must have carried substantial weight with the Government and the Department of the Environment was the general state of the North-West despite a substantial measure of Government financial aid channelled through the other strand of regional development policy. As John Ardill described it in *The Guardian*: 'The North-West has a "distinctly poor" environment and the general quality of life is often below that of any other English region. Yet its people and industry are paying more into the public purse than the region gets back in public spending.'[4]

When the Joint Team began work, three priorities of some significance were soon recognized: (a) that the pre-eminent aim of the strategic plan was to produce a framework plan in line with the second of its Terms of Reference – a desired future pattern of social, environmental and economic development for the region, concerned with the use and conservation of regional and national assets, aimed at establishing and maintaining in the region a quality of life in balance with the rest of the country; (b) that this improvement in the quality of life 'must mean, above all, the improvement of living conditions in the urban areas'; and (c) that the strategy was to be regarded as only the first stage in a process of continuous planning for the region.

With regard to time horizons associated with this desired future pattern for the region, the Joint Team were of the opinion that:

> The strategic plan is therefore not a once-for-all blueprint for the future – though it looks forward twenty years or so, towards the end of the century. Significant years in the plan-making process are 1981 and 1991 . . . This does not mean that the 1970s are any less important than the 1980s or 1990s. It is a question of reconciling long-term objectives for the region with the action to be taken in the relatively short-term future.[1]

In this respect nine major regional issues were identified as a result of the wide range of issues presented to the Consultative Committee in the form of the Issues Report. These included the following:

(a) The desirable levels of population growth and economic growth – including the likely balance of labour supply and demand.

(b) The opportunities and needs of the region, and the resources required to meet them, including possible changes in the Exchequer grants system to local authorities.

(c) Improvement of the urban environment, including reduction of pollution; the balance between clearance and rehabilitation of housing; and the needs of the under-privileged in the inner cities.

(d) The strengths and weaknesses of the regional economy – including the relationship to the national economy; the mobility of industry; and the balance between manufacturing and service employment.

(e) Transport – including the balance between public and private transport; access to urban facilities, industrial sites, the ports, and the countryside; and the large-scale environmental effects of the region's airports.

(f) Regional open land – including modifications of the green belts; possible regional parks; and the reconciliation of the recreational needs of townspeople with agricultural and other uses of open land.

Having examined a number of indicators of performance with respect to the quality of life, indicators which are susceptible to action in the public sector, the Joint Team found a disturbed and disturbing picture. As A. G. Powell, the Team's Director, has noted:

... the North-West has the worst river pollution in the country ...; the highest incidence of derelict land; the highest general standardised mortality rates; the highest infant mortality rates. The interrelationship between some of those is immediately apparent. It has the lowest proportion of doctors to population – in spite of the need. It has the highest ratio of pupils to teachers anywhere in the country and the lowest availability of open country for recreation ... The North-West is also near worst, not only in the areas which have been declared 'black areas' under the Clean Air Act (1956) but are not yet subject to smoke-control order, but also in the ratio of footpaths and ... urban open space per head of population.[3]

Merseyside, despite massive injections of capital during the past three decades, he suggests, sticks out like a sore thumb. Because of the capital-intensive nature of this investment, the unemployment problem in the area has not materially altered.

Yet there have been great successes ... in reorientating the structure of industry in the North-West. Textiles, coal and the ports have been success-fully contracted without serious labour troubles (this is a good example of planning for decline) and at present we find that structurally, at least, the North-West is not badly placed.[1]

Whilst the region as a whole increased its population by about 160,000 people between 1961 and 1971, the cities of Manchester and Liverpool each lost 20 per cent. As Powell argues, the effect of this situation is that the rich parts of the country are getting richer and the poor parts are getting poorer in terms of resources available for environmental improvement.

The eight long-term objectives for the region, as spelt out in the *Strategic Plan*, reflect this concern. These were split into two distinct groups: operational objectives (relating to the form of the plan) and regional objectives (relating to the substance of the plan). The four operational objectives were:

(i) feasibility – to formulate a strategic framework and a set of policies which are realistic in the light of the powers and resources available to the agencies implementing the plan;

(ii) flexibility – to provide a strategy which is flexible enough to cope with uncertainty about the future;

(iii) implementation – to identify and make explicit the policy requirements of alternative strategies; and

(iv) efficiency – to use the region's financial and natural resources as efficiently as possible.

The four regional objectives were:

(v) environment – to improve the quality of the environment;

(vi) economy – to improve the economic performance of the region;

(vii) social fabric – to raise the quality and levels of provision of facilities and services as a means of improving the quality of life; and

(viii) communications – to improve communications systems.

Each of these objectives were considered to be provisional. In other words, as the plan-making processes proceeded, the Joint Team recognized that each would need redefining, to be modified in some way, or even eliminated as untenable or undesirable. During the preparation of the alternative strategies and their evaluation, each objective was scrutinized and given a 'weighting' as to its relative importance. These refined and reworked objectives numbered twenty-three, grouped under six headings:

Quality of life (seven objectives)
Conservation (five objectives)
Economic efficiency (two objectives)
Costs (two objectives)
Flexibility (four objectives)
Feasibility (three objectives)

The 'weights', corresponding to 1981 and 1991, were expressed in percentage terms. For example, the highest weighted quality of life objective for 1981 was 'to locate development so as to provide the best possible choice of jobs'[1]. This carried a weighting of 10·55 per cent. The criterion by which this objective was to be evaluated corresponded to 'access to jobs with allowance for travel time and distance'[1]. For 1991, however, the weighting was lowered (i.e. accorded less priority) to 8·55 per cent. The highest weighted objective in the quality of life section for 1991 carried a weight of 8·80 per cent, which was 'to locate development so as to provide the most attractive living environment'[11]. The criteria, or indicators – as the Joint Team labelled them – for this particular objective concerned '(a) landscape features, and (b) absence of pollution, noise, etc.'[1]. It is perhaps of interest to note that the highest weighted objective for both 1981 and 1991 was concerned with economic efficiency: 'To locate development so as to provide the best possible choice of labour supply for firms and business enterprises'[1]. The weights were 15·25 per cent and 12·80 per cent respectively. The indicator to evaluate whether or not each alternative strategy measured up to this objective was 'access to population with allowance for travel time and distance'[1]. (The nine objectives categorized under costs, flexibility and feasibility were not weighted.) According to the Report: 'The objectives of the plan and how best to achieve them were were kept in mind throughout the whole process, though in the later stages of formulating regional policies, this became more a matter of judgement than of measurement.'[1]

So, having defined the problems facing the region as being largely environmental and concerning especially the quality of life in the urban areas, and derived a set of provisional objectives by which alternative strategies could be evaluated, the Joint Team set to work (a) to estimate the scale and magnitude of, and (b) to prepare provisional policies for, the nine broad issues outlined earlier.

(a) Population and economic growth

We find that the most intense pressures on the environment, particularly in the North-West, result more from the achievement of rising personal standards than from the numerical growth of population . . . We arrive at the view that as far as future population is concerned, *the North West does not have to plan for inevitable, large-scale growth; or set out to attract large-scale growth.*[1] [Italics added.]

The 'best guess' estimates of population growth in the region to the turn of the century suggested that the increase would be of the order of $\frac{1}{2}$ million (from $6\frac{3}{4}$ million in 1971 to $7\frac{1}{4}$ million by 2001). Employment was expected to remain fairly stable. In these respects the Joint Team made four critical working assumptions about the future of the North-West:

(i) a continued declining share of the country's total population and employment;

  (ii) some absolute increase in the total population though probably
       much smaller than in the past, and with continued net migration
       out of the region;
 (iii) continued economic growth in the U.K. and the region, but with
       minimum impact on employment levels; and
 (iv) a rough balance between jobs and workers in the 1970s, with the
       later prospect of some imbalance.

(b) Opportunities, needs and resources of the region

These were of two kinds: the identification of and need to put to best
use existing opportunities, and the correction of existing or potential
deficiencies. The opportunities were considered to be: (i) the population
itself, (ii) the sophisticated and accessible supply of labour available, (iii)
the wide choice of job opportunities, (vi) the higher education facilities,
and (v) the new infrastructure, particularly the motorway network.

The assessment of needs was related specifically to issues of public
expenditure, and to what was susceptible to direct action by local and
central Government. This consisted of inter-regional comparisons of
quality-of-life indicators: housing, pollution, wealth, medical and social
facilities, education, recreation and cultural facilities. The Team drew
the conclusion that: '. . . Other aspects of life in the North-West may
well compensate for the deficiencies. Nevertheless, we reach the conclusion that the quality of life in the region is not 'in balance with the rest
of the country'[1].

Issues concerning resources were principally concerned with problems
of financial resources in the public sector. The assumption was that,
although the private sector was clearly critical, regional policies for the
North-West 'will largely rely on the public sector to trigger off investment by the private sector'. It was estimated that local and central
government spent about £650 million a year in the region, of which
65 per cent was current expenditure and 35 per cent capital (about £238
million per annum). However, the Joint Team were of the opinion that
on the basis of the available information levels of public expenditure in
the region were low compared with other regions. Also that the North-
West was experiencing a net outflow of public funds to the rest of the
country.

In this respect, the Joint Team delved into relations between central
and local government, and in particular the financial links between them
in the form of the rate support grant (R.S.G.). The object of this grant,
a simple transfer payment or subsidy from the Exchequer to local authorities, is to bring the level of rateable income in each authority up to the
national average. The fact that most authorities in the North-West were
in receipt of this grant indicates that their incomes from local rates were
substantially lower than the average income from rates in the U.K.

The problem with the R.S.G. is that it provides no financial incentive to local authorities to increase the size of their rateable value. Any additional development – commercial, industrial, or residential – only serves to lower the financial contribution made by central government. For those areas like the North-West with substantial social or economic problems, the R.S.G. – as the principal source of central government finance to local authorities – provides little in the way of additional finance to set about their resolution. The Joint Team's findings in this respect were unequivocal: 'We recommend improvement of the rate support grant . . . but conclude that the most effective way to stimulate rapid action to improve the quality of life generally, and the appearance of the urban areas in particular, is through the machinery of specific grants.'[1] Three main types of specific grant were suggested: social (for people), physical (for places), and transport (for movement). On top of these specific grants, the Joint Team proposed a special regional fund, to be administered at the regional level by 'any regional body which advises on resource allocation'[1]. The object of this special fund would be to provide 'a means of helping to adjust the balance of spending priorities in the interests of the region as a whole'[1].

(c) Improvement of the urban environment

In line with the Joint Team's basic quality of life objectives, their concern for existing urban environments, and their findings as to the state of the North-West generally, it is perhaps not surprising that the principal issues raised as to public expenditure priorities should reflect these concerns. The approach suggested was that the needs of each sector should be evaluated against current commitments to determine the magnitudes of mismatch: standards of performance should be set on a sector by sector basis, reasonable time-scales should be determined for their fruition, and assessments of the likely effort required estimated. However, because of the short-term 'life' of the Joint Team, they could only concentrate their attention on one particular regional issue – that of pollution ('shown by our assessment of needs to be a field in which this region is worse off than any other')[1].

Their assessment of the scale of public expenditure necessary 'to secure significant improvement in this decade'[1] in the satisfactory resolution of the regional pollution problem was between £308 and £441 million, at 1972 prices. The greater proportion would be necessary to improve the region's rivers, about £245 to £352 million. Reclamation of derelict land would accommodate between £40 and £55 million, and smoke control between £23 and £34 million. If the trend in the proportion of public expenditure already spent on pollution control continued, the Joint Team estimated that by 1981 this would amount to about £185 million, i.e. an estimated short-coming of between £123 and £256 million.

Since a major contributor to the region's river pollution problem was seen to be sewerage, the Joint Team proposed that priority should be given to the extension of available specific grants for sewage treatment schemes. With regard to environmental pollution, proposals envisaged a concentration of effort and funds for the reduction in air pollution and reclamation of derelict land.

The 'poor urban environments' in particular, were considered to be those areas primarily in the Mersey Belt, and to a lesser extent in North-East Lancashire and the towns of Northern Cheshire. The Joint Team were also of the opinion that the local authorities in these areas were generally 'those with most to do'[1]. The proposal was for concerted action on a co-ordinated basis, to aim at the improvement of the physical environment as a whole in these areas, rather than piecemeal improvements. To set about this task the Joint Team proposed a separate but permanent 'environmental grant' to supplement and top up other specific grants from central government. 'Such a grant, together with extended urban aid . . . fits in with our more general views on the subject of resources and the idea of broad freedom of action for local authorities to deal with 'people', 'places' and 'movement'.'[1]

(d) The state of the regional economy

Issues concerning employment in the region stressed the idea that its poor record was not because of a predominance of nationally declining industries, nor because of insufficient national-growth industries. Rather, two explanations were offered: (a) because of the failure of the region's existing industries to increase the size of their labour pools (industrial efficiency, competitiveness, relative cost differentials of new locations, and levels of investment being mentioned), and (b) because of the bias towards the attraction of capital-intensive, rather than labour-intensive, industries built into current regional economic policies. As the Joint Team noted, apart from the Regional Employment Premium (R.E.P.), such policies have been addressed primarily to structural problems rather than problems concerning industrial efficiency and competitiveness. The policy proposals to which the Joint Team drew attention were: (i) the need for direct subsidies to reduce operating costs, primarily labour (a strengthened R.E.P.); (ii) a redressing of the balance between capital and labour incentives; and (iii) flexible arrangements for training and retraining labour.

Employment in the service sector, primarily offices, was also considered to be of some importance. As the Joint Team put it: 'It would be desirable to align government policy on office location with other government policies on the distribution of industry and location of employment . . . The recent extension of assistance to service industries is a welcome step in this direction.'[1]

(e) Transport

Four basic problems existed: (i) the role of public versus private transport; (ii) the implications of a changing emphasis from building major urban roads to traffic management schemes; (iii) the region's two airports; and (iv) the ports.

The Joint Team clearly placed a good deal of emphasis on the findings of the two major land use/transport studies conducted in the region: Merseyside (MALTS) and Greater Manchester (SELNEC). Although only the proposals for upgrading commuter rail lines into Liverpool and Manchester were formally endorsed, the Joint Team proposed that both the Liverpool Terminal Loop system and the controversial Picc-Vic underground link in Manchester were 'most important'[1].

Proposals for improving and upgrading a number of inter-urban roads were assessed against two criteria: an estimate of the economic return, and its value to the regional strategy. The roads which satisfied this assessment procedure were, in the main, ouside the Liverpool–Manchester belt, consisting of three principal routes and by-passes up to 1981 and five to 1991.

The assessment of the role of the two regional airports drew the conclusion that competitive expenditure between Manchester and Liverpool Airports 'is a potential waste of regional resources and should be avoided'[1]. The assessment of the region's ports concentrated on problems of improving transport access.

(f) Land use

Because the *Strategic Plan* is predominantly a physical strategy, it is not surprising that land and the use of land figured large in the Joint Team's deliberations. 'The fundamental need is for all the remaining open land in the region to be committed in one way or another by a positive open land policy designed to fit in with the broad physical pattern of development.'[1]

The principal components of this policy proposal were related to an assessment of the impact of, primarily, agriculture, forestry, amenity and outdoor recreation, airport noise and safety, scientific conservation, water conservation, mineral extraction, rural settlement, and green belts. Of these, outdoor recreation and green belts were considered to be of particular importance, together with the National Parks and the need for regional parks.

THE PHYSICAL PATTERN OF DEVELOPMENT

Having estimated the scale and magnitude of the issues facing the future development of the region, and prepared statements of policy as a guide, the Joint Team set about the task of preparing a framework for the physical pattern of development on which to hang these policies. This meant deriving a set of alternative possible strategies for the North-West in line with the objectives set for its development. The process was in reality more complex than this; the sequence of setting objectives, deriving alternative strategies and evaluating them was undertaken *three* times. On each occasion the objectives, alternatives, and the evaluation procedures were reworked, redefined, and eventually refined.

Initially six alternative strategies were considered, based on two recurrent themes which dominated the work, moulded thinking behind the strategies, and were reflected in the chosen strategy for the location of population and employment in the region. These were: (a) concentration or dispersal, and (b) intervention to reinforce or counteract market forces and trends in urban development. In other words, should future development be concentrated in a few, specific locations – in existing urban areas or greenfield sites – or should it be more dispersed? Should present trends be reinforced (e.g. the movement of population from large urban areas like Liverpool or Manchester) or should they be counteracted (e.g. by controlling new development in more rural areas)?

These six 'rough and ready' alternatives encompassed both concentration and dispersal as focal points, but in various forms and in different degrees. These six were (see Figure 3.1, page 43):

(i) to concentrate future development along the existing east–west Mersey–Manchester belt;
(ii) to concentrate future development in and around the Central Lancashire New Town of Leyland–Chorley (C.L.N.T.);
(iii) to concentrate future development in a new city in South Cheshire;
(iv) to disperse future development around the peripheries of Merseyside and Greater Manchester;
(v) to concentrate future development in the Lancaster–Morecambe area; and
(vi) to concentrate future development just outside the region at Deeside.

Each alternative was evaluated in both objective (quantifiable) and subjective (qualitative) terms, to see how each fared against the objectives set for the region. This evaluation consisted of an assessment of the feasibility, flexibility and costs of each, and for their impact on three main groups:

(a) people occupying new areas of development;
(b) people continuing to live in existing urban areas; and
(c) less privileged people occupying inner areas of Liverpool and Manchester.

These six were then refined down to *four* 'second-cycle' alternatives – two concentrated, two dispersed. These were in turn evaluated against the reworked objectives and with reference to their policy implications. These policy implications consisted of six broad areas for evaluation: the impact of each alternative with respect to (a) the current Development and Intermediate Area status of the region, (b) the rapid improvement of the urban environment, (c) open land and countryside, (d) existing land commitments, (e) infrastructure requirements, and (f) the release of land for future development.

This short list of four consisted of a Mersey Belt strategy, a C.L.N.T. strategy, a South Cheshire new city strategy, and a peripheral growth strategy around Liverpool and Manchester. The second-cycle evaluation suggested that the regional objectives and resolution of the main issues facing the region would be best served by an emphasis on a *more concentrated* than dispersed pattern of development. Several reasons were put forward:

(a) it offers more all-round advantages, particularly in relation to job choice, access to urban facilities, the level of provision of those services, public transport, and aiding the less privileged;

(b) the disadvantages are more a matter of physical form and structure than accommodating actual numbers of people;

(c) the maximum possible resources are needed in the Mersey Belt, where the main environmental problems are to be found;

(d) large-scale expenditure on infrastructure in the existing urban areas is needed in any event, whatever the spatial pattern;

(e) the best prospects for regional employment growth are associated more with existing centres of industry than with new locations;

(f) the potential of the three New Towns in the Mersey Belt could be exploited to the full in support of current regional policies.

The Joint Team's preferred pattern of development, however, had a principal constraint – the physical capacity of the Mersey Belt to contain new development. So any strategy based on concentration would involve some element of dispersal. The relative 'mix' between the two involved what the Joint Team called 'options', and in particular options based on three main variables: the location of employment, the level and rate of population displacement from existing urban areas, and the release of land for new development. But the ability to control and influence each of these varies considerably. Control over the location of employment in the region is more than limited. The region being both a Development Area and an Intermediate Area means that industry can locate pretty much where it wants. Similarly with controls over population displacement. Both are notoriously difficult, if not impossible, to predict with any measure of certainty or detail. The principal means of control, and by no means as effective as some local planning authorities have hoped (as the findings of the inquiry into the Greater London Development Plan admirably illustrated), was seen to be the amount and rate of land released for housing development. As the Joint Team puts it:

> In examining the options the main element over which control can be exercised is land release. And since the green belt is the most important single policy element diverting the market forces for development, it is the green belt areas where major changes from the present situation are potentially most influential. This works both ways – relaxation of green belt or extensions of it . . . reinforcing the positive use of open land and channelling development.[1]

The preferred emphasis was translated into a third set of alternatives, called 'major strategic options'[1]. These were based on the need for choosing between:

(i) location of jobs – either spreading out from the conurbations or retention/expansion within them;
(ii) population displacement – either moderate or high; and
(iii) land release – either releasing green belt land where market pressures are strongest, or restricting land release, pushing development further out from the conurbations.

These alternatives were then evaluated against six broad categories or reworked objectives (based on the nine issues originally outlined):

(a) impact on job choice and employment growth;
(b) impact on access to urban facilities and their improvement;
(c) impact on the channelling of resources for environmental improvement;
(d) impact on the less privileged;
(e) impact on improved public transport; and
(f) impact on open land.

The evaluation procedure employed both qualitative and quantitative forms of assessment. This took the form of trading off the costs against the benefits associated with each broad option. The preferred alternative was based on a set of five interrelated preferences or biases. These were: first, a preference for 'an optimum distribution'[1] of employment growth, rather than 'maximisation of regional growth'[1]; second, a relaxation of green belt policy along selected corridors around the conurbations; third, an extension of green belt restrictions around these corridors; fourth, a preference for 'an underwriting of the importance of the city centres' and the need for selective locations in the Mersey Belt as centres of employment; and finally, a preference for greater use of public transport.

It was, therefore, assumed that (a) concentration of jobs in or near existing urban areas, and particularly the Mersey Belt, would bring 'a wider spread of regional benefits'[1]; (b) corridors of urban development around the conurbations would 'promote greater use of public transport, provide better access to job opportunities and bring benefits to parts of the inner-cities'[1]; and (c) extending the green belt, notably to the south of the Mersey Belt, would favour both new development in the corridors and urban regeneration, 'thus frustrating housing demand in some highly attractive living areas'[1].

On the basis of these preferences and assumptions, the Recommended Physical Pattern of Development proposed indicative ranges in both population and employment to 1991. The population changes are summarized in Table 3.1.

Table 3.1

| | 1971 Population (000's) | Changes in Population to 1991 | | | |
| | | Low | | High | |
		(000's)	(%)	(000's)	(%)
Greater Manchester	2,720	−70	−2·6	−10	−0·4
Merseyside	1,652	−32	−1·9	+8	+0·5
Mersey New Towns	354	+133	+37·6	+175	+49·4
Total Mersey Belt	4,726	+31	+0·7	+173	+3·7
Rest of Lancashire	1,257	+24	+1·9	+62	+4·9
Rest of Cheshire	609	+68	+11·2	+78	+12·8
Grand Total*	6,592	+123	+1·9	+313	+4·7

* excluding Furness and High Peak
Source: S.P.N.W., Table 10.2; G. H. Peters (1975).

On these assumptions the Mersey Belt would account for about a quarter of the total population increase on the low estimate, and over half on the high estimate. How these preferences, assumptions and indicative ranges of population change were translated into the strategy is illustrated in Figure 3.2. What the Joint Team referred to as twelve strategic areas of land release for urban development were chosen. Four of these are existing New Towns, and six are corridors for development – two to the east focusing on Liverpool, three to the north and west, and one to the south focusing on Manchester. Those areas not identified as green belts, National Parks, or Areas of Outstanding National Beauty (A.O.N.B.), were scheduled as areas for the operation of positive open land policies and local growth. In summarizing their proposals, the Joint Team concluded that the strategy was not a once-and-for-all blueprint plan for the North-West. Rather they saw the role of the strategy as being more a starting point for (a) the implementation of central and local

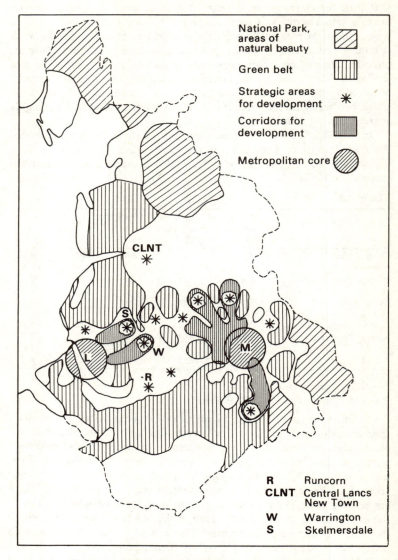

National Park, areas of natural beauty

Green belt

Strategic areas for development

Corridors for development

Metropolitan core

CLNT

S

L

W

R

M

R   Runcorn
CLNT Central Lancs New Town
W   Warrington
S   Skelmersdale

Figure 3.2—Source: 'S.P.N.W.', *The Surveyor* (1975).

government policies within the region, and (b) 'continuous planning'[1] – a need for the constant monitoring and review of the assumptions and policies contained in the plan with those policies and programmes actually affecting the region, and hence altering the basis of the plan. As they conclude:

> It has been an attempt to understand how the region works – seeking fresh information; challenging established views of what is 'good' for the region; and all the time trying to explore the region's possible future in a realistic way. The plan is made up partly of predictions, partly of hopes and partly of efforts to persuade those concerned to adopt new policies or take particular courses of action.[1]

NOTES AND REFERENCES

1. North West Joint Planning Team, *Strategic Plan for the North West*, H.M.S.O., 1974.
2. *The Guardian*, 21 December 1973.
3. A. G. Powell, 'Regional Policy and Sub-Regional Planning in the North-West', in M. Sant (ed.), *Regional Policy and Planning for Europe*, Saxon House, 1974.
4. 'North West 2000', *The Guardian*, 7 May 1974.

QUESTIONS FOR DISCUSSION

1. How does the *Strategic Plan for the North-West* differ from previous strategic plans?
2. Outline the principal recommendations of the S.P.N.W.
3. Should a long-term strategic plan be concerned with the resolution of current problems? Discuss with reference to the S.P.N.W.
4. 'Rather than see carefully worked out strategies for development well outside the metropolitan areas gather dust in pigeon holes, regional planners prefer to concentrate development as best they can inside those areas where the willing agents are.' Suggest reasons why this might be the case in the North-West.
5. Outline the methodology employed by the Joint Team in preparing the *Strategic Plan*.
6. What were the 'major strategic options' which the Joint Team identified? Discuss the principal implications with regard to the North-West.
7. The concept of 'trade-off' was an important feature of the preparation of the *Strategic Plan*. What was meant by this concept? How was it employed in the planning process?
8. How does regional strategic planning differ from regional economic policy?

9. In the light of the S.P.N.W., discuss the possible directions regional strategic planning could take in the future.
10. In the context of the S.P.N.W., what is meant by:
    (i) 'strategic plan',
    (ii) 'corridors of development',
    (iii) 'environmental improvement'?

The Greater London Development Plan
A regional plan for a congested area

Regional policy is generally thought of as a method of alleviating or controlling economic problems in depressed and underdeveloped parts of the country. Obviously this is an important aspect of regional economic policy and indeed has in the past often dominated thinking in this field. It is not the only aspect, however. Economists and politicians are becoming increasingly concerned about regulating the growth of the more *prosperous* areas of the country. The reasons for this interest is easily understood; these dynamic regions provide many of the nation's exports, act as magnets to mobile factors of production (and hence divert them from distressed regions) and contain a large proportion of the country's population. Those living in these regions are being increasingly subjected to congestion, overcrowding and pollution as immigration continues and industrial production expands. In this case study we look at attempts to control the economy of such a dynamic region and consider in detail the Greater London Development Plan (G.L.D.P.).

Geographically the Greater London region is small but it still contains approximately one in eight of the population of Britain. For this reason planning for London has a comparatively long history and as far back as 1939 a major report, the Barlow Report[1], recommended a gradual outward movement of workers from the capital because of increasing overcrowding and a deteriorating environment. Here we are concerned with much more recent developments and in particular with the G.L.D.P. and the subsequent public inquiry which carried out an extensive economic appraisal of the G.L.C.'s planning proposals.

The major planning exercise began in 1963 with the formation of the Greater London Council (G.L.C.) under the London Government Act of that year. According to the legislation in the Town and Country Planning Act (1947), then in force, the G.L.C. was committed to draw up a 'town plan' outlining its intended long-term policy – this involved constructing a cartographical impression of the physical layout of the region at some pre-determined date in the future. In itself this was a task of immense proportions but the job was complicated considerably in 1968 when a change in the law (under a new Town and Country Planning Act) called not for a cartographical plan but for a written statement of the future physical, social and economic structure of the city – a 'structure plan'. The G.L.C. was to present the authority's long-term objectives and to provide a critical assessment of the feasible strategies to achieve them. From this unhappy marriage a somewhat bastardized document emerged in 1969; a seventy-seven page *Statement*[2], which was neither a structure plan nor a town plan in the strict sense. It was primarily literary but did contain nine large-scale maps.

The *Statement* (along with supporting technical material was examined in public inquiry by a committee under the chairmanship of Sir Frank Layfield. We consider both the economic underpinnings of the G.L.D.P. itself and the subsequent comments and criticisms laid against it by the Layfield Committee. The latter is of particular interest not only because of the scale of the inquiry, but because it represents an attempt to appraise a large regional planning exercise in a systematic way, employing economic techniques where appropriate.

AN OVERVIEW OF THE G.L.D.P.

London is not only a large city but also an economic region in its own right. Its growth and expansion pattern both affects the economies of surrounding regions and is also in turn influenced by them. This clearly complicates the planning process, planners needing to consider both the effects of their policies on other regions and at the same time modify their own ideas in the light of what is happening elsewhere. In particular the economy of the G.L.C. is closely interconnected with that of the South-Eastern planning region. The importance of this interdependence was recognized in the G.L.D.P. and brought to the fore in some of the comments of the Panel of Inquiry. Indeed some of the proposals regarding employment policy later needed substantial revisions following the publication in 1971 of the *Strategic Plan for the South East*[4].

The freedom of action enjoyed by the G.L.C. in drawing up their plan was severely limited by the political controls imposed upon it by the 1963 Act. In particular considerable power was left in the hands of thirty-two large borough councils and the City of London which retained control over certain spheres of activity within their own areas (see Map 4.1). This lower tier of government, for example, was left with responsibility for local housing policy (e.g. density of development, etc.) leaving the G.L.C. with general directive powers with respect to the movement of population between boroughs and to New Towns outside the region's boundaries.

Given these constraints the basic strategy of the G.L.D.P. can be summarized thus:

> It is the council's intention to do everything within its power to maintain London's position as the capital of the nation and one of the world's great cities. It intends to foster the commercial and industrial prosperity of London

Map 4.1. The Boroughs of London.
Source: *The Economist,* 16 December 1972, p. 77.

and its cultural status, especially in respect of these functions for which a London location may be regarded as essential. The social conditions which the people of London are to enjoy will depend upon this prosperity and the flourishing economy and culture which it should produce.[2] (p. 10).

To fulfil this strategy the Council set out seven quite explicit aims[2] (p. 12):

1. To liberate and develop, so far as planning can, the enterprise and activities of London, promoting efficiency in economic life and vitality in its society and culture.
2. To treasure and develop London's character – capital of the nation, home and workplace of millions, elements of the British tradition.
3. To conserve and develop London's fabric, of buildings, spaces and communications, protecting the best while modernizing what is out of date or inferior.
4. To promote a balance between homes, work and movement as principal elements upon whose relationship London's overall prospects depend.
5. To participate in necessary measures of decentralization and help forward the part that London plays in national and regional development.

6. To encourage continual improvement in metropolitan environments and make them congenial and efficient in the service of London's people.
7. To unite the efforts of all who can help to realize these aims and to give new inspiration to the onward development of London's genius.

Given these primary aims, the G.L.C. considered its most pressing objective must be to stem the outflow of population which had been a feature of the capital's post-war history – the region's population falling from 8·6 million in 1939 to 7·4 million in 1971. The arguments for deliberately encouraging out-migration, advanced initially by Barlow and supported by subsequent commissions, centred around the dominant position the city enjoyed in the South-East which, it was felt, prevented adjacent regions from realizing their full economic potential. There were also feelings in the 1950s and early 1960s that London was too large *per se* and in particular was imposing excessive social costs on those living in the city. The G.L.C. countered this view by arguing that the continued depopulation, especially of inner areas, would have adverse effects on the local economy. It felt that the city was being deprived of young, skilled, well-educated people, families with young children and workers with the best prospects, leaving behind the old, the less skilled and disadvantaged. To continue a policy of depopulation would place increasing burdens on those remaining without increasing their ability to meet them. It was strongly argued in the *Statement* that the continued decline in the resident labour force would, by 1981, reduce the efficiency of many London-based firms, increase inflationary pressures and place considerable strains on community facilities as more workers travel in to work from other regions.

In terms of publicity the most controversial aspect of the G.L.D.P. was its transport proposals. (This concern was also registered at the later inquiry where 90 per cent of the objections to the plan related to transport.) The G.L.C. recognized the increasing problems of traffic congestion in the city but after carrying out an extensive transport survey found that the root cause was not only the traditional one of commuter concentration during the morning and evening peaks (indeed only about 12 per cent of commuters travelled to work by motor car) but also involved *through* traffic at other times of the day. To deal with the considerable volume of non-stopping traffic the G.L.D.P. contained proposals for the construction of a series of 'ring and radial' urban motorways. Three ring motorways were envisaged, three miles, seven miles and twelve miles respectively from the city centre, with a fourth, further out, to be planned by the Department of the Environment (see Map 4.2 for details). In addition, the radial system was to be improved with several new urban motorways proposed, together with the up-grading of a number of existing trunkroads.

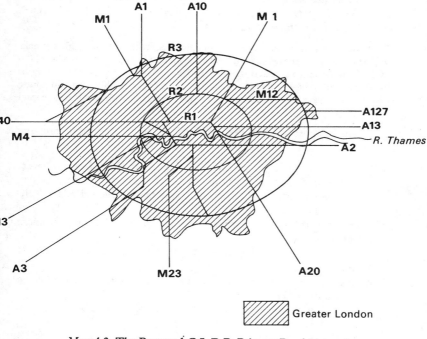

Map 4.2. The Proposed G.L.D.P. Primary Road Network.
Source: adapted from G.L.C. *Statement*[2].

The *Statement* says very little about public transport. This may in part be due to the fact that the G.L.C. only took full responsibility for London Transport in 1970. The reason for the private transport bias in the G.L.D.P. may also be attributed to the basic philosophy of the planners. For example, in his evidence to the Panel of Inquiry, the G.L.C.'s Chief Planner, Mr. Bernard Collins, stated: 'Public transport can offer a reliable basic service but there are circumstances when it is not a satisfactory or realistic substitute for a car for most people of the kind envisaged as forming the future population of London.' (It has been suggested by at least one author[6] that the G.L.C.'s planners were worried that the valued middle-class high income-earners would only stay in London if they could own and use a car.)

Housing figured prominently in the G.L.D.P., and this is not surprising considering the accommodation problem in London. Much of the capital's housing was old, 69 per cent was built before 1920, and there was considerable overcrowding in some quarters. The age of housing and the intensity of occupation meant that the condition of property was deteriorating and the general environment in the immediate neighbour-hood suffered correspondingly. The policy set out in the G.L.D.P. was intended to alleviate this problem:

> The council's overriding aim, in collaboration with the borough councils will be to secure a progressive improvement in the environment so that London as a whole becomes a much more attractive place to live in than it is at present; a place which offers better opportunities for its children and young people to develop, which meets better their needs for physical and mental recreation.[2] (p. 11).

Six firm proposals were put forward to solve the most pressing problems:

1. 'First priority' was to be given to the eradication of slums, over-crowding and 'lamentable domestic environments'.
2. To provide as many new dwellings as a good standard of environ-ment will permit.
3. 'First Priority' was to be given to improving the 'Housing Problem Areas'.
4. To attempt a gradual redistribution of population, especially to Outer London.
5. Encouragement was to be offered to private enterprise and housing association building.
6. To provide for a continued flow of 20,000 residents a year to expanding towns.

The G.L.C. hoped to increase the choice and variety of housing by encouraging private development as well as public building. An alter-native motive was the need to spread the cost of modernizing the housing stock and to reduce the financial burden that extensive public building programmes place on rate- and tax-payers. The encouragement of private enterprise and housing association activity was also seen as a way of stemming the outflow of higher-income earners from the city.

THE LAYFIELD PANEL'S COMMENTS ON THE G.L.D.P.

The Layfield Panel concluded: 'In short, we consider the Metropolitan Structure Plan in its present form dangerous and largely useless, and we recommended that you (i.e. the Secretary of State for the Environment) should not approve it.' Why was this the finding of the Panel of Inquiry? Clearly the reasons were not entirely economic in nature but nevertheless in social cost-benefit terms many of the G.L.D.P. proposals did not offer a reasonable return for the high financial costs involved. We look at the general criticisms levelled by Layfield first, and then consider the more detailed comments of specific proposals.

Four fundamental criticisms were made of the overall approach adopted by the G.L.C. in the preparation of their plan.

1. The plan was over-ambitious. The G.L.C. attempted to alter settled population trends and to forecast the demand and supply conditions for labour into the distant future. The Panel of Inquiry contended that the G.L.C. did not have the instruments to influence the former (at least not in the short term) nor the information to forecast the latter. The plan would, therefore, have benefited by being more limited in its scope.

2. The general treatment was not always consistent. The Committee felt that the G.L.C. tended to concentrate on specific proposals – especially those where it had full information and in areas where its powers were strongest – to the detriment of other problems.

3. There was a failure to relate information to policy. The Panel complained that the G.L.C. frequently made inadequate use of the data it had collected from surveys and on occasions totally ignored it, with the result that certain policy proposals appeared independent of all available information. In some cases the policies appeared to run directly counter to those suggested by the data supplied.

4. There were general problems of defining objectives and aims and in relating them to policy. The Panel complained that it found difficulty in discovering the precise aims of certain policies while in other instances the stated aims were so general and woolly that they could be interpreted in any way the reader wished.

These are obviously criticisms of the planning method employed; for more fundamental comment of the economic shortcomings of the G.L.D.P. we need to consider specific proposals.

(a) The appropriate population for London

Perhaps the most significant divergence of opinion between the Panel of Inquiry and the G.L.C. was over the appropriate policy to pursue with regard to the future population of the city. The implications of whatever policy was adopted would affect all other components of the plan. As indicated earlier, the G.L.C. favoured a policy of population stabilization but the Layfield Panel disagreed strongly with this. The Panel felt 'that continuation of decreases in employment and population at recent rates will produce a greater increase in net benefit than would a retardation in the decline.'

In some senses the approach adopted by the Inquiry appears to be very negative. Instead of assessing the merits of the policy advocated in the *Statement* it appraised the effects of the prevailing situation of net out-migration. For example, we find the Report stating: 'No evidence was presented to us which shows that a higher than normal proportion of people in the higher-paid jobs is leaving London, nor that prosperous firms are moving out more readily than non-prosperous firms, nor, if they are, what effect this has on incomes, nor that the fall in employment ... is affecting income per head.'

In addition to arguing that a reversal of existing migration is inappropriate for London the Inquiry Panel also questioned the methods the G.L.C. had suggested to achieve their objectives. The G.L.C. assumed they could stop the outflow of employment, and hence population, by taking over from the Board of Trade responsibility for floor space controls and possibly by convincing central government to relax I.D.C. policy in London. Not surprisingly the Layfield Committee felt this approach would be ineffective and suggested several other more efficient ways of regulating employment levels, including:

   (i) the rehabilitation of worn-out areas;
  (ii) offering prepared sites for industry and offices;
 (iii) improving public transport to increase access to jobs;
 (iv) improving public transport to assist the movement of goods;
  (v) developing new sources of employment such as tourism.

Basically the Layfield Report was critical of the basic G.L.C. policy on population and employment in the city. In addition, it was felt that the G.L.C. should adopt a more realistic approach towards the policy instruments available to it and, once the basic principles upon which the optimal population was to be determined had been settled, the G.L.C. should utilize the very much wider range of powers at its disposal rather than rely on floor space controls.

(b) London Housing

The Panel of Inquiry supported the G.L.C.'s idea that as many houses as possible should be constructed to meet those problems which could not be met by population dispersal policies. However, it rejected any proposal that more dwellings should be built simply to slow or reverse the outflow of population from the region.

In particular the inquiry team were concerned about a number of quite serious omissions in the housing chapter of the *Statement* and they questioned whether the G.L.C. proposals actually represented a strategic plan for housing at all. There was also an extensive criticism of the inadequate degree of integration of the G.L.C.'s housing proposals with those for transport, employment, etc. In addition the Panel felt that no adequate econometric forecasts had been made of the future housing needs of London, in its view a rather crude estimation procedure being a poor substitute for sound forecasting.

Besides being extremely critical of G.L.C.'s housing policy, the Panel of Inquiry also attempted to be constructive. In particular it suggested that much greater co-operation was needed between the G.L.C. and the lower-tier borough authorities. The Committee thought that such co-ordination might be achieved by establishing a 'strategic housing authority'. This new body was to be responsible both for the construction of new housing in London (since 'the interests of the boroughs and the G.L.C. are, quite naturally, in conflict') and for the regulation of a common waiting list for public housing. Such an authority should be able to speed up the programme of redevelopment in London and pursue an active policy of rehabilitation. A co-ordinating body was thought particularly necessary because redevelopment and rehabilitation both create problems of decanting (i.e. housing those formerly living in the area being improved).

With regard to the detailed aspects of housing policy, the Layfield Committee felt that where the social benefits of extending residential estates into Green Belt areas exceeded the social costs, this should be done. The Report states: 'Land shortage is no reason for building to unsatisfactory environmental conditions.' The Panel were also sceptical about the role private enterprise could play, arguing that the size of its effort would depend upon market conditions and these may not correspond to the needs of those seeking accommodation. It also felt that the G.L.C. would have to use compulsory purchasing powers if substantial improve- ments were to be forthcoming in the private rented sector.

The Panel drew specific attention to the possible loss of cheap housing in redevelopment schemes (both public and private), especially if they were in inner London. The redevelopment of, say, Mayfair, would not raise serious problems but if multi-occupied privately rented houses in Paddington were demolished and replaced the Panel felt that: 'The authorities should not delude themselves that the problem [of poor housing] will be solved if the new development contains new residential units to replace those units lost, unless it can assure itself that the new units will be suitable for the displaced households and be rented at rents they can afford.'

(c) London's transport policy

The G.L.C.'s transport proposals were the most controversial aspect of the G.L.D.P. judging from the public response to them. The Inquiry felt that the proposals set out in the *Statement* failed to provide a co-ordinated future transport policy for the city – in particular they did not bring together in harmony policies in four major fields: public transport, traffic management, road improvement and the environment.

The Panel of Inquiry was particularly concerned with the emphasis placed upon urban motorways to solve the city's traffic congestion problems. Although not opposed to urban motorways, especially if their design and construction had negligible effects on the environment, the Committee was concerned about the detailed proposals.

Firstly, there was a fear that the construction of these roads would *generate* additional traffic in the centre of London and the G.L.D.P. did not suggest that any supplementary traffic management policies were likely to be implemented to control this growth. The Report states: 'Without strict management and stringent restraint, it is clear that there would be a gradual deterioration in the quality of life and in the economic efficiency of London.'

Secondly, Layfield felt that even if appropriate controls were implemented, the triple ring road programme was excessive: 'Such a lavish provision of orbital roads will in our view either result in a situation in which they are not utilised to their full capacity, and hence be a waste of valuable resources, or alternatively, and more probably, they will encourage inessential movements by road which otherwise would either not take place or would take place by some alternative mode.' In other words with appropriate traffic management schemes the proposed motorway was too large and without controls it would generate excessive and unnecessary traffic in the inner London region.

Given these quite major criticisms, the Panel proceeded to prune the G.L.D.P.'s road building programme. A cost-benefit appraisal was used to look at the merits of each ring road and, although the return on all of them was extremely low (5·4 per cent in the case of the best, the inner motorway box) and would not normally justify the construction of any of them, the Panel did retain some of the original network (see Map 4.3). In particular, the inner ring road *was* approved despite the numerous objections raised against it on environmental grounds by local pressure groups and by individuals likely to be adversely affected. The Panel's justification for the motorway box was that the C.B.A. study was not comprehensive, in particular 'important environmental advantages gained by the canalization of traffic that would otherwise use secondary and local roads remains unaccounted for in money terms'. This conclusion was subsequently subjected to very heavy criticism in the press and academic circles. As one commentator[7] put it: 'It is not building Ringway 1 that will enhance the environmental quality of central London, but traffic restraint and environmental traffic planning.' In the event the Department of the Environment, after initially accepting the modified Layfield scheme, abandoned an urban motorway solution to the G.L.C.'s transport problems as being too expensive.

The Panel of Inquiry paid considerable attention to the public transport system in the capital. It agreed with the G.L.C.'s statement of intent 'to improve public transport in all possible ways' but was critical of the lack of any firm proposals to achieve this basic objective. The Layfield

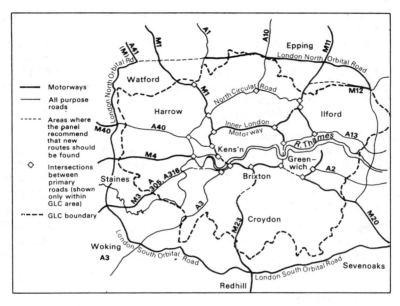

Map 4.3. The London Road Network proposed by Layfield.
Source: adapted from *The Economist*[5].

Committee agreed that a constructive and carefully prepared strategy for public transport was necessary for three reasons:

1. Many people, especially among the poorer sections of the community, relied upon public transport as their sole means of transport.
2. Public transport reduced the need for new roads by diverting travellers away from the private motor car.
3. Good public transport makes the regulation of private transport much easier and considerably more acceptable.

To achieve the required degree of reliability, cheapness, convenience and comfort, the Panel felt that there was a need to create a common financial framework within which the various public transport operators functioned, and combined with this a common set of goals, aims and objectives was essential. To improve operating efficiency, the bus network should be thoroughly reviewed and modified where necessary. As the Report stated, 'only by ensuring that all concerned have common aims, and we are not deterred from pursuit of those aims by financial considerations peculiar to individual parties, can matters be improved.' To meet these needs a co-ordinating central body for transport policy was advocated, together with sufficient financial funds to achieve the desired goals, even if the latter meant subsidizing operating as well as capital costs.

The control and regulation of London's traffic by management schemes was an important component of the Panel's overall approach. 'Without strict management and stringent restraint, it is clear there would be a gradual deterioration in the quality of life and in the economic efficiency of London.' It recommended that three types of traffic restraint measures should be employed in the city:

(I) An extended system of parking controls.

(II) The canalization of traffic (by one-way systems, no through roads, signposting, etc.) on to routes where vehicles were likely to cause the minimal environmental damage and the least impedance to public transport.

(III) The introduction of area licensing.

To ensure that these measures were applied correctly, the Panel suggested that the G.L.C. improved its traffic forecasting techniques and monitored the effects of the various policies adopted.

CONCLUSIONS

The G.L.D.P. was an exercise in economic planning for a thriving if congested region of the country. The actual plan was itself open to a wide range of criticisms, many of which were quite damning, but nevertheless the attempt to plan for a region with a population of over 7 million people, together with its importance as a commercial, communications and industrial centre was not a waste of resources. The plan was a pioneering effort to control the economy and development of one of Britain's major conurbations and has certainly provided invaluable information and knowledge which will be used elsewhere. This is of particular importance since the enactment of the 1972 Local Government Act, which has established a number of Metropolitan Authorities throughout England and Scotland with similar responsibilities to the G.L.C. They can only benefit from the experiences gained in London.

The greatest strength of the exercise was that it clearly revealed where the pitfalls in this type of planning are likely to occur. The Layfield Inquiry was of considerable importance because it pointed to the need for planning objectives to be specific – those of the G.L.C. were extraordinarily vague in places – and for the resultant policies to be a logical extension of the objectives. It was also important because it clearly revealed that the new type of structural planning introduced under the 1968 Act could only be construed as urban economic planning. As one commentator[8] has put it: 'The selection and evaluation of alternatives is an economic process; and therefore much of the content of structure plans, however expressed, is recognised as raising economic issues.' The G.L.D.P. was therefore innovatory, being the first genuine attempt to plan in economic terms the future development of a thriving urban region in Britain.

REFERENCES

1. Royal Commission on the Distribution of Industrial Population, *Report*, Cmnd. 6153, H.M.S.O., 1939.
2. Greater London Council, *Greater London Development Plan Statement*, G.L.C., 1969.
3. Department of the Environment, *Greater London Development Plan*; *Report of the Panel of Inquiry*, H.M.S.O., 1973.
4. South-East Joint Planning Team, *Strategic Plan for the South-East – A Framework*, H.M.S.O., 1971.
5. 'It's that Motorway Box Again.' *The Economist*, 24 February 1973.
6. D. Wilcox, 'The Greater London Development Plan', in J. Hillman (ed.), *Planning for London*, Penguin, 1971.
7. C. D. Foster, 'An Inquiry into the Layfield Inquiry', *The Times*, 21 February 1973.
8. C. D. Foster and C. M. E. Whitehead, 'The Layfield Report on the Greater London Development Plan', *Economica*, November 1973, pp. 442–54.

QUESTIONS FOR DISCUSSION

1. What were the institutional difficulties confronting London planners in the preparation of a development plan?
2. Explain in your own words the underlying objectives of the G.L.D.P.
3. What were the Layfield Panel's main criticisms of the G.L.D.P.?
4. What proposals did the G.L.D.P. contain regarding the provision of housing? Critically appraise these proposals.
5. 'The main shortcoming of the London plan was its limited consideration of national and wider regional developments.' Discuss this view of the G.L.D.P.
6. Briefly explain the following with respect to the G.L.D.P.:
   (i) 'structure planning', (ii) 'the motorway box', (iii) strategic housing authority', (iv) 'co-ordinating central body for transport policy'.
7. Compare and contrast the differing views of the G.L.C. and the Inquiry Team towards the appropriate population policy for London.
8. The G.L.D.P. transport proposals have been criticized for being too

much private-car orientated. Outline the main proposals and discuss the validity of this criticism.

9. What was the significance of the G.L.D.P. exercise for urban and regional economists?

10. An article in *The Economist* of 8 December 1962 'North to Elizabetha' (pp. 989–90) suggested that many of the regional economic problems of the North and of London itself could be greatly reduced by removing the capital of the country to a new city, Elizabetha, situated on open land between York and Harrogate. In what ways might this be preferable to the G.L.D.P. proposals? In what ways would it be less satisfactory?

The Regional Policy of the Common Market
Regional policy in Europe

This case study explains and comments upon the regional economic policies which have been pursued by the European Economic Community (E.E.C.) and more specifically upon the Thomson Report. E.E.C. regional policy is of particular interest for several reasons. First, Britain's membership of the Community means that traditional policies adopted towards our less prosperous regions must now be integrated into the overall regional policies of the E.E.C. This suggests that certain policy instruments used to induce investment and development into the depressed areas may conflict with the wider objectives of the Community, and consequently must be replaced by instruments which accord with E.E.C. rules and regulations. This is not necessarily an argument against membership of the Community on regional policy grounds (in that respect this study attempts to be neutral) because once in the E.E.C. much larger funds become available to tackle our regional difficulties. Secondly, E.E.C. regional policy is of interest in itself because it represents an attempt to overcome internal economic difficulties within several countries by a concerted and unified approach on their part. Although each member state retains control over its own regional policy, the overall scale of assistance to the depressed areas and the way in which it is distributed, is in many ways determined by the Community as a whole. Thirdly, some of the policy tools employed by E.E.C. members to tackle their own regional problems are worth considering as potential instruments for British regional programmes. Finally, there is the problem that membership of the E.E.C. may have adverse effects on regional income and employment disparities within Britain; in particular the peripheral areas of Scotland, Wales and Northern Ireland will be further away from the centre of a European market than they were from the centre of the U.K. market.

The development of an E.E.C. regional policy has been extremely slow despite quite marked disparities in income levels both between nations and within them. The earlier European Coal and Steel Community, initiated in 1951, was little concerned with regional problems although it was recognized that from time to time assistance would be required in areas where technological change resulted in unemployment. This was not realy a regional policy as much as a recognition that *ad hoc* actions would be required on occasions when a region suffered unemployment as a result of technical changes.

The Treaty of Rome, upon which the European Economic Community is based, makes no specific provision for a common regional policy, although the issue is not entirely ignored. In the preamble to the Treaty we find each member state 'desirous of strengthening the unity of their economies and of ensuring their harmonious development by reducing the differences existing between the various regions and by mitigating the backwardness of the less favourable'. The members agreed to promote throughout the Community 'a harmonious development of economic activities'.

These words of intent were strengthened by some of the clauses in the Treaty proper. Although the Community is committed to economic policies which do not distort competition, there are a number of exceptions and we find under Article 92 of the Treaty that it is permitted to give 'aids intended to promote the economic development of regions where the standard of living is abnormally low or where there exists serious under-employment'. In addition, during the transition period leading up to the Community becoming fully functional, countries could request authorization to use appropriate policies necessitated by 'difficulties which may seriously impair the economic situation in any region'. Also, both the common transport policy and the prohibition of discriminatory support tariffs may be relaxed on regional grounds. For a more detailed account of the regional policy content of the Treaty of Rome the reader is directed to Flockton[1].

THE REGIONAL PROBLEMS OF THE E.E.C.: AN OVERVIEW

Although economic growth was impressive in the E.E.C. during the 1960s there were considerable disparities between countries and within them. The regional disparities at the beginning of the last decade were considerable, and we find that *per capita* income in 1963–4 for the richest country in the Community, France, was some 73 per cent higher than that of the poorest, Italy. This difference is relatively small, however, when compared to the disparities between the richest and poorest regions *within* the member states. The differences in *per capita* income between the richest and poorest regions in France, Italy and Germany were 280 per cent, 243 per cent and 156 per cent respectively. We are concerned primarily with intra-national difference in economic performance.

These overall figures tend to hide a number of particular and, in many cases, longstanding regional problems in certain countries. The situation in Italy is perhaps the best known of these problems. Whilst the north of

Italy is relatively prosperous and enjoyed rapid economic growth through-out the past decade, the south or Mezzogiorno, has suffered from low incomes and slow industrial growth. Some 40 per cent of the labour force is still employed in agriculture in the South and there is severe unemployment. Over the whole of the Mezzogiorno *per capita* income is less than two-thirds of the national average and in three provinces – Basilicata, Molise and Calabria – it is respectively 57 per cent, 54 per cent and 49 per cent of the national average[2]. The emigration of workers from the area to the North and to other E.E.C. countries has to some extent offset the unemployment problem, but it does mean that the most dynamic and skilled elements of the labour force are leaving the area and making it even less attractive to investors.

France also has severe regional problems although different in nature from those of Italy. Many of the traditional industries in France have gone into decline, while other areas are still predominantly agricultural and consequently do not enjoy great prosperity. The population and distribution and patterns of migration in recent times have added to the regional problems. The predominantly agricultural regions of the west and south-west are seriously underpopulated relative to the rest of the country, and there is a continual outflow of labour as modernization of farming results in the displacement of agricultural workers. In contrast the Paris conurbation constitutes about 2 per cent of the country's land area but contains 19 per cent of the nation's population – this is causing serious problems of congestion. Congestion creates social costs in the form of pollution and inconvenience which have adverse effects on the local population. The Paris region is prosperous and therefore a natural draw for the agricultural unemployed but the continued inflow of people imposes severe social costs which is a cause of concern.

The Benelux countries are a relatively small part of the Community but still suffer from their own regional problems. Belgium has experienced considerable problems in her coal-producing areas which, due to their relatively high production costs, have tended to suffer as E.E.C. coal production has centred on the low-cost field of France and Germany. The difficulty has been compounded by political complications. The main coalfields are in the French-speaking Walloon area of the country, whereas the new growth centres tend to be in Flemish-speaking regions. Holland's demographic problem is congestion and overpopulation although its agricultural sector's growth still lags behind the rest of the economy. Its regional problems are, nevertheless, fairly minor.

Germany has the obvious regional problems that West Berlin is geographially isolated from the remainder of the country, but apart from this the main difficulties involve the partition of Germany and the cutting-off of several areas from their traditional markets. In addition some of the primary producing industries, notably coalmining and iron-ore mining, have gone into decline and this has had adverse effects on several areas of the country, notably the Ruhr and Saar. Finally, parts of Germany are agricultural and suffer from low levels of investment, below-average incomes and an outflow of population.

In the early years of the Community there was some improvement in the internal position of most of the E.E.C. countries, although this was as much the result of the extremely rapid pace of economic growth within the E.E.C. as to any attempt at regional policy. In 1971 the National Institute of Economic and Social Research compared *per capita* income in the 'peripheral' regions of each member state to the national average

Table 5.1

	1958	1963	1968
France	N.A.	85·2	86·2
West Germany	89·5	93·1	93·2
Italy	73·0	73·1	71·6
North Netherlands	85·5	86·4	87·0

Source : N.I.E.S.R.[3] (p. 57).

for selected years (see Table 5.1). The term 'peripheral' is, broadly, defined to mean lying furthest from the main centre of population and, in particular, from the densely populated strip running from North-West Italy to the Belgium coast (the so-called 'Golden Triangle').

The table suggests that regional disparities in *per capita* income diminished in each country between 1958 and 1968 with the exception of Italy. Two points should be noted before accepting these findings. First, the table hides some income differences by considering simply 'peripheral' regions relative to the national position – it ignores, therefore, the disparities between the richest and poorest areas in each country. This averaging out could conceal substantial income differentials. Second, although the table indicates that the position in Italy deteriorated over the decade this sheds a slightly unfair light on the situation. Italy had the fastest growing economy in the E.E.C. during the 1960s but much of this was concentrated in the northern part of the country. The south did enjoy considerable economic expansion, however, and, although its relative position deteriorated *vis-à-vis* the rest of Italy, *per capita* income in the Mezzogiorno increased compared to the Community as a whole.

To put the position of the United Kingdom in perspective, the comparable figures for the country in the years 1958, 1963 and 1968 were 82·8 per cent, 82·7 per cent and 83·5 per cent respectively. Regional disparities within the U.K. had diminished over the decade but this was only at the cost of considerable economic aid being given to the regions (some £240 million in 1967). The improvements within the Community were gained from a much smaller programme of assistance.

THE EVOLUTION OF REGIONAL POLICY IN THE E.E.C.

The onus of dealing with regional problems has been primarily on the shoulders of national governments. The 1960s was a period of high economic growth rates for E.E.C. members and attention was concentrated on ensuring continued increases in national incomes. Little was done during the period to remove regional disparities but this is not to say policy recommendations were not made. The 1960s saw a large number of reports written (e.g. the *Birkelbach Report* (1963) and the *Bersani Report* (1966)) and speeches given (e.g. by Jean Rey (1968) and Hans von der Groeben (1969)) which touched on regional policy but it was more notable for two important memoranda dealing with the subject.

The first of these, the *Memorandum on Regional Policy in the Community* was presented in 1965 and had the dual purpose of:

(a) bringing about agreement within the Community on the objectives and methods of regional policy, and

(b) co-ordinating the means of action of the member states and, to the extent of their jurisdiction, of the Community Institutions, for the realization of these objectives.

The Memorandum clearly showed the thinking of the Community with regard to regional policy at the time. The objectives of the proposals were the promotion of agricultural and industrial regions suffering from structural difficulties in order to reduce disparities between their economic performance and that of the more prosperous areas within the Community. The case for a regional programme for each *ensemble économique cohérent* was made. These programmes were intended not just to alleviate income differentials between regions, but also to assist in the wider aims of the E.E.C. by ensuring an improved allocation of economic resources. To assist in these programmes it was recommended that the territory of the Community be divided into four separate categories depending upon their economic circumstances (i.e. (i) underdeveloped – mainly agricultural – regions; (ii) regions of basic industry in decline; (iii) prosperous urban concentrations; and (iv) frontier regions. The idea of these four categories was in 1965 not new; it had been voiced at a Conference of experts on regional economics convened in Brussels four years earlier.) Each of the strata could then be assisted in an appropriate manner.

The second Memorandum from the Commission of the European Community appeared in October 1969 under the rather long-winded title 'Proposals for the organisation of means of action relation to Regional Development in the Community and a Note on Regional Policy in the Community' (for more details of this document see Despicht and Flockton[4]). The proposals contained in this memorandum differed from those of the 1965 document – the economic situation in Western Europe had changed and economic union within the Community had progressed further. Regions within the E.E.C. were divided into three groups:

1. Industrialized Regions. These would be densely populated with a low proportion of agricultural workers. These regions represented about 16 per cent of the land area of the Community and about 42 per cent of the total population lived in them. These regions included a substantial part of the population and land areas of Germany and the Benelux countries but accounted for less than 10 per cent of the territory of France and Italy and only 30 per cent and 20 per cent of their respective populations.

2. Semi-industrialized Regions. These would have less than 15 per cent of their active labour force in agriculture. These regions covered about a third of the land area of the Community and accounted for about 40 per cent of the population. Substantial parts of Germany, Italy and the Netherlands come under this classification but it only embraced about 20 per cent of the population and land area of France.

3. Agricultural Regions. These regions were characterized by a low density of population and an agricultural labour force of between 20 per cent and 40 per cent of the total number of workers. This type of region accounted for over half the area of the E.E.C. and about a quarter of the population. The areas falling into this category were mainly in France (70 per cent of the land area) and Italy (55 per cent of its territory).

The Memorandum recommended the creation of an advisory and co-ordinating committee, the Standing Regional Development Committee, to carry out annual examinations of national regional problems. Development plans submitted by member states could be discussed and community aid could only be given after consultations with the Committee. The Committee should work in conjunction with the European Investment Bank, which supplies one observer member of the Committee. (The Bank itself oversees the provision of financial assistance for investment projects, the majority of which have been in Southern Italy) and should attempt to co-ordinate the regional policies of the various member states. In addition to this body a new fund was advocated, the Regional Development Rebate Fund, which would assist in the financing of projects of giving interest rebates from the Community Budget.

The 'Note' incorporated within the Memorandum (mentioned in the title of the document) was concerned with the philosophy behind the Community's thinking on region policy. This it saw as the creation of conditions where economic structures can adapt to changes in technology to enable a harmonization of economic levels. This implied the creation of employment and the provision of necessary infrastructure in the depressed areas and also the reduction in 'social costs' – pollution, etc. – in prosperous regions. The Note defines four main types of regional policy available to the Community:

(a) regional aids and the rational allocation of budgetary expenditures to take account of regional disparities;
(b) the harmonization of economic legislation in response to the freeing of locational constraints on economic activity;
(c) regional development plans and the creation of harmonized sets of regional statistics;
(d) the choice of priorities.

The realization that the rapid economic growth enjoyed by the Community throughout the 1960s was unlikely to be repeated in the 1970s called forth further discussions on regional policy, and this in turn was followed by a number of proposals in 1971 and 1972. In October 1971 the member states of the Community agreed to adopt by the beginning of 1973 a system which would (a) define the regions in need of assistance, (b) restrict the level of assistance which may be given to other areas and (c) reorganize the types of assistance permitted so that they are quantifiable and hence comparable with each other.

The idea was that the Community should be divided into central and peripheral areas, the latter consisting of Southern Italy, West and South-West France, Berlin and regions bordering on East Germany. The remainder of the land area of the E.E.C. was to be classified as central. In these central areas any aid given to investors would be limited 'by a single intensity ceiling expressed in net subsidy equivalents'. A common method of evaluating different types of assistance was used to calculate this ceiling. Also the 20 per cent ceiling initially suggested was a maximum, levels of assistance within the central regions varying beneath this figure as circumstances demanded. In addition assistance given nationwide to investors (for example the 100 per cent tax-free first year allowance in the United Kingdom) was excluded from the calculations.

Implementation of the Commission's proposals has however been extremely slow. The main measures to date are the restriction of regional assistance to central areas and some agreement on other policies which have yet to be finalized.

The enlargement of the Community provided the opportunity for a reassessment of regional policy and this in turn produced the so-called Thomson Report, *Report on the Regional Problems in the Enlarged Community* (May 1973). Mr. George Thomson was one of the two British Commissioners appointed following entry into the Community and was at that time responsible for Regional Policy. This Report stated: 'It cannot be said that economic activity throughout the Community has developed evenly, nor has expansion been geographically balanced.' The Report is as much concerned with congested and overcrowded regions as with the depressed ones:

> The physical poverty of the under-privileged regions is matched only by the mounting environmental poverty of the areas of concentration. The pressure on housing, the miseries of commuting on overloaded roads, or overcrowded trains, the pollution of the air and the water – all these developments mean that the environmental case for closing the geographical gaps is as powerful a one for those who live in the so-called prosperous areas of the Community as it is for those in the poorer regions.

To assist in this objective the Report recommended that efforts be made to obtain agreement on common policies to reduce congestion and overcrowding in the prosperous areas.

Despite the attention paid to the congested regions by Thomson, however, it was the proposals for the depressed areas which attracted the greatest attention both in the press and amongst academic commentators. This is not altogether surprising considering the background to the Report and the overall trends in E.E.C. policy taking place at the time.

The Paris summit meeting of October 1972 had re-affirmed the decision to press on with Economic and Monetary Union (E.M.U.) within the Community. It was realized, however, that

> There can be no European union without economic and monetary union, and no economic and monetary union without an adequate and effective regional policy backed by a fund with substantial resources ... The Heads of State or of Government agreed that a high priority should be given to the aim of correcting, in the Community, the structural and regional imbalances which might affect the realisation of Economic and Monetary Union.

In other words the creation of a monetary union would deprive the member states of one of their most powerful economic tools, the power to change their exchange rates, and a rational and substantial regional policy would be required to provide some degree of compensation for this. This fear was that monetary union would be to the benefit of the already prosperous areas of the so-called 'golden triangle' and to the detriment of peripheral regions. (For further details of the proposed monetary union, see Presley[5]). In the sense that this period also witnessed the geographical expansion of the Community, a regional policy was required to enable some new members – notably Britain – to recoup money paid into the Common Agricultural Fund.

The Thomson Report emphasized the need for both a Regional Development Fund, which it suggested should be established on 31 December 1973, and a Regional Development Committee to supervise the harmonization of national regional policies (for details see Stubenow[6]).

The fund, it suggested, should be used to give both grants and interest payment rebates on loans for specific schemes devoted 'entirely to medium-term and long-term developments'. As was subsequently pointed out in *The Economist*[7], these proposals were rather conservative and the effectiveness of regional policy depended 'upon picking the right schemes to support'. The criteria for regions eligible for assistance were three-fold:

1. A persistent and high level of unemployment.
2. Low or relatively declining regional income per inhabitant.
3. Net outward migration.

A major criticism of these three criteria is that they are all static. The argument centres around the fact that it is the rate and direction of change in unemployment, income and migration which determines the condition of a regional economy and not the absolute level of these variables. As Derek Ezra[2] has observed with regard to E.E.C. regional policy generally, 'The criteria . . . will need to be dynamic so as to eliminate anomalies created with the passage of time.' This is a particularly strong argument if the harmonization of regional policy is designed to compensate for the loss of the devaluation weapon. It was felt that many countries were experiencing regional unemployment problems because their currencies were overvalued. If this was the case, then the removal of the power to devalue their currencies would make it difficult to alleviate the problem. The replacement regional policy should, therefore, approximate as closely as possible to changing the exchange rate; since overvaluation of a currency affects the *rate* at which unemployment rises, it should be this rate of increase, rather than the base level of unemployment, which determines the need for regional assistance. In other words, if the members of the E.E.C. are no longer allowed to devalue, then the alternative of regional assistance should be related to the changes in unemployment, income, migration, etc. if it is to be at all effective.

The need for a co-ordinating body with overall responsibility for regional policy within the Community was also apparent from the diversity of policies pursued by member countries (see Allen[8] for a detailed account of these differences). The Thomson Report was important not only because of its support for the Regional Development Committee but also because it documented the different types of regional policies being used by members and also assessed their relative effectiveness. All members used the traditional incentive tools of capital grants, state loans, tax and interest allowances, etc. in various combinations; but three – Britain, France and the Netherlands – also employed negative methods to discourage further investment in their congested regions (for more detail see Ezra[2]). Italy had a number of specific bodies to implement her regional policies and for encouraging more investment in the south;

of these the Cassa per il Mezzogiorno is perhaps the best known. In addition there were direct instructions for the large national companies to create employment in the south (and less direct instructions to private companies to do likewise). Also something like 60 per cent of new public investment was allocated to the Mezzogiorno. In Britain the Regional Employment Premium was being used directly to subsidize employers of labour in Development Areas while in the Netherlands a premium of £1,170 was paid to firms for each worker employed in designated regions. If the E.E.C. was to become an economic union with a community regional policy, clearly some co-ordination of national policies would be required.

THE UNITED KINGDOM AND E.E.C. REGIONAL POLICY

In 1973, the six original members of the E.E.C. – France, Germany, Italy, Belgium, the Netherlands and Luxembourg – were joined by the United Kingdom, Eire and Denmark. For the United Kingdom membership had important implications for her regional policy. Throughout the 1960s the U.K. had been spending considerably more on regional assistance than other member countries (e.g. between five and ten times as much as France) without being conspicuously more successful. A fundamental difference in the U.K.'s regional problems compared with, say, Italy, was that she was attempting to convert and redevelop areas which were already industrialized – this explained the policy of bringing 'work to the workers' rather than *vice versa*. Italy, on the other hand, had the problem of introducing industry into backward areas which were predominantly agricultural and this was impossible to achieve without some inter-regional shifts in the working force. This meant that the U.K. was seeking a somewhat different type of regional policy than the traditional problem area of the Community, Italy[9].

Membership of the European Economic Community affects British regional policy in four fundamental ways.

First, membership of the E.E.C. is likely to have some effect on the national rate of economic growth within the United Kingdom. In as much as regional problems of low incomes and unemployment are at least partly a function of the national growth rate, joining the E.E.C. should reduce regional disparities *if* faster economic expansion is a result. This is a long-term effect, because it will take time for membership to influence the performance of the national economy and then take a further period for this to work its way through to the regions.

Secondly, membership of the Community may have a direct effect on the amount of private sector investment going to the depressed areas of the U.K. The Development Areas and other assisted regions are chiefly peripheral and away from the main centres of communication and commerce. Inside the E.E.C. these regions become even more isolated from the main European centres and from potential markets – especially from the 'Golden Triangle' – and will therefore be much less attractive to investors. It is also possible that the prosperous areas of the country will appear less attractive to foreign capital which may go to Continental sites now offering access to both the mainland European markets and the United Kingdom.

Thirdly, membership of the Community reduces the policy instruments available to the United Kingdom Government and the strength at which they may be applied – the suggested 20 per cent maximum assistance permitted in central areas can be cited as an example of this. The problem extends beyond a simple consideration of explicit regional policy into other spheres. The Community transport policy, for example, does not permit subsidies for railway services in depressed areas in normal

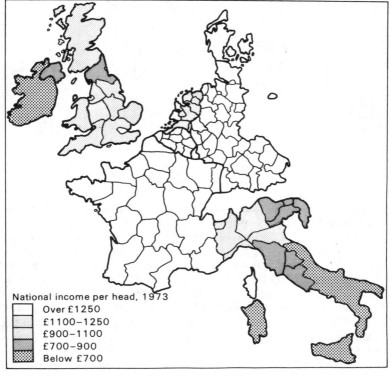

National income per head, 1973

- Over £1250
- £1100–1250
- £900–1100
- £700–900
- Below £700

Map 5.1. The poor.
Source: *The Economist*[7].

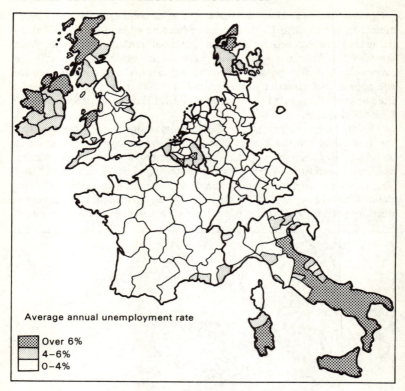

Map 5.2. The jobless.
Source: *The Economist*[7].

circumstances but such subsidies have been given in the past as part of the United Kingdom's implicit regional assistance programme.

Finally, there are the direct implications of the Community's regional policy for the U.K. – in this context we pay particular attention to the implications of the Thomson Report for the U.K. regional policy. The Report suggested that the Regional Fund should be divided out on three main criteria, *per capita* income, migration and unemployment, but it has been argued that this is against the interests of the United Kingdom[10]. Maps 5.1, 5.2 and 5.3 are based upon information contained within the Thomson Report and illustrate the income, unemployment and migration situation for members of the E.E.C. It is clear that, with the exception of Northern Ireland and parts of Northern England, there are no British regions with particularly low incomes, although the country is relatively poor compared to the majority of the Community. The 'cut-

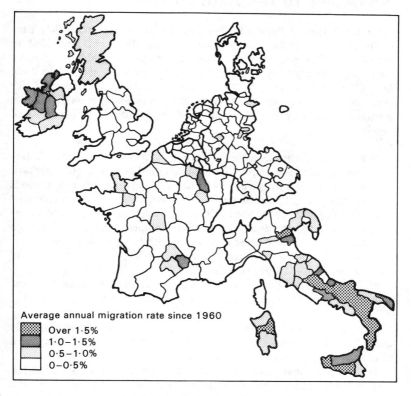

Map 5.3. The migrants.
Source: *The Economist*[7].

off point' for aid is therefore very important in the British context. We also find that unemployment in Northern Ireland, North Scotland and parts of Wales is comparable with that in Southern Italy but that other areas enjoying Development Area status are relatively well off and this would limit the assistance they would be entitled to. (The figures are slightly distorted since they are based upon data averaged over a number of years and tend to understate the situation in some areas of Britain where traditional industries have declined rapidly in the early 1970s). Migration patterns would suggest few problem areas in the U.K. except for Scotland. This is a very poor criteria for regional assistance, however, since migration out of Scotland tends to decline if the macro-economic situation in England deteriorates, but this does not mean the Scottish economy is thriving – usually the reverse is true.

POSTSCRIPT TO THE THOMSON REPORT

Since the Thomson Report further negotiations on regional policy have taken place within the Community. Initially these were intended to modify the Thomson proposals and make them acceptable to member states but subsequently a completely new package emerged. In 1974 M. Albert Borschette, Mr Thomson's predecessor as Commissioner responsible for Regional Policy, brought out a paper recommending that assistance should be given on the basis of four different categories of region:

1. Southern Italy, Greenland, Eire and Northern Ireland. These regions should be eligible for the amount of assistance their national governments were giving them in January 1975 although projects costing over £12·5 million should be vetted by the Commission.
2. The French assisted areas, the Italian Alps and the United Kingdom's Development and Special Development Areas. These should be eligible for 30 per cent assistance with investment projects.
3. West German border areas and parts of Denmark. These should be eligible for 25 per cent assistance.
4. Central Areas (including the U.K. Intermediate Areas). These areas should have assistance limited to 20 per cent.

He argued that all 'opaque' types of regional aid (i.e. those not easily quantified or assessed) should be phased out except in very exceptional circumstances approved by the Commission.

Borschette's suggestions were not very popular with member states, mainly because they were too rigid and the definitions used somewhat arbitrary, and in the negotiations at the end of 1974[11] a new package began to emerge. Regional assistance was to be much smaller than the £1,000 million per annum that was mentioned in 1973 and a fund of £542 million was to be established to assist depressed areas over a three-year poiod. (The E.E.C. always expresses finance in 'units' and hence conversion into sterling does not produce round figures). The money was to be allocated amongst member countries rather than by pre-determined categories of region; Italy would receive about 42 per cent, the U.K. 28 per cent and Eire 6 per cent. (The total sum was revised in January 1975 to £625 million of which the U.K. would get about £125 million). Certain criteria were to be used to show which projects could be given assistance from the Fund and the first six months of 1975 were set aside to draw these up. It was felt better to have definite criteria so that applications for funds could be dealt with much more rapidly than if each project had to be individually assessed by the Commission – in any case they did not have the expertise to do the latter. It appears that the eventual criteria will be of a negative nature designed to show which projects are ineligible rather than *vice versa*. The suggestions are that schemes involving prestige investments and creating only minimal employment should be rejected, as should those designed to subsidize declining industries producing luxury goods. This seems to leave a very small range of industries eligible for aid. Because of the need to spend time drawing up these criteria it seems unlikely that more than £60 million or so of the Fund will be allocated in 1975.

REFERENCES

1. C. Flockton, 'The emergence of a regional policy for the European Communities', *Loughborough Journal of Social Studies*, No. 8, November 1969, pp. 29–45.
2. D. Ezra, 'Regional Policy in the European Community', *National Westminster Bank Quarterly Review*, August 1973, pp. 8–21.
3. 'The Economic Situation: the Common Market', *National Institute of Economic and Social Research Economic Review*, August 1971, pp. 54–61.
4. N. S. Despicht & C. Flockton, 'Regional Policy in the European Communities: the Shadow of Integration', *Loughborough Journal of Social Studies* No. 9, June 1970, pp. 24–41.
5. J. Presley, 'The Implications of Economic and Monetary Union on National Policy', *Loughborough Papers on Recent Developments in Economic Policy and Thought*, No. 4, 1975.
6. W. Stubenow, 'Regional Policy in the E.E.C.' in M. Sant (ed.), *Regional Policy and Planning for Europe*, Saxon House, 1974.
7. 'Europe and Britain's Regions', *The Economist*, 21 April 1973, pp. 55–64.
8. K. Allen, 'European Regional Policies' in M. Sant (ed.), *Regional Policy and Planning for Europe*, Saxon House, 1974.
9. G. Magnifico, 'Regions of Discontent', *The Guardian*, 15 November 1971.
10. H. Beggs and J. Allan Stewart, 'Britain and E.E.C. Regional Policy', *Political Quarterly*, Vol. 44, 1973, pp. 58–69.
11. 'Who's the poorest of them all?', *The Economist*, 28 December 1974, p. 34.

QUESTIONS FOR DISCUSSION

1. How do the regional problems of the member states of the E.E.C. differ?

2. 'E.E.C. policies are needed to deal with intra-national as well as international disparities in income.' Explain the significance of this statement and compare the magnitudes of the two problems.

3. What were the main recommendations of the 1969 Memorandum on regional policy?

4. Summarize the ways in which the United Kingdom's membership of the E.E.C. affects her regional policy.

5. Critically appraise the recommendations of the Thomson Report.

6. One of the main problems in drawing up a regional policy for the Community has been to define the geographical areas which are to be assisted. Outline the different proposals which have been made over the years to solve this problem.

7. Critically appraise the use of *per capita* income, migration and unemployment as measures of a region's economic condition.

8. 'Community regional policy must deal with prosperous areas as well as depressed ones.' How have individual members of the E.E.C. attempted to tackle the economic problems of their prosperous regions? How has the E.E.C. attempted to tackle the problem?

9. What is the relationship between European Monetary Union and E.E.C. regional policy as proposed in the Thomson Report? Why is regional policy unlikely to be an adequate replacement for the loss of economic freedom which E.M.U. implies?

10. 'E.E.C. regional policy depends as much on political criteria as it does on economic principles.' Discuss this statement using past E.E.C. proposals on regional policy as illustrations.